An Opera Miscellany

Everything you never knew about opera for buffs and bluffers

Robert Weinberg

Foreword by Lesley Garrett CBE

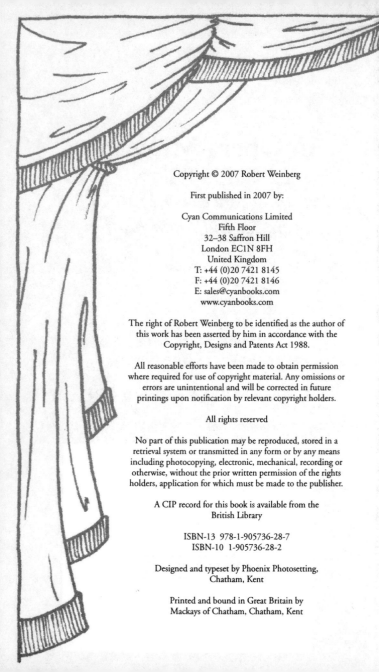

First published in 2007 by:

Cyan Communications Limited
Fifth Floor
32–38 Saffron Hill
London EC1N 8FH
United Kingdom
T: +44 (0)20 7421 8145
F: +44 (0)20 7421 8146
E: sales@cyanbooks.com
www.cyanbooks.com

A CIP record for this book is available from the
British Library

ISBN-13 978-1-905736-28-7
ISBN-10 1-905736-28-2

Designed and typeset by Phoenix Photosetting,
Chatham, Kent

Printed and bound in Great Britain by
Mackays of Chatham, Chatham, Kent

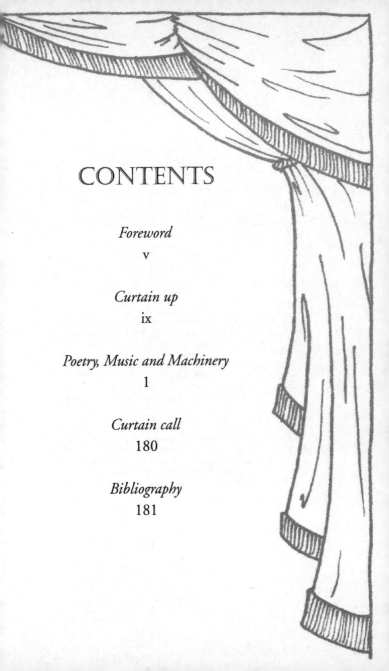

CONTENTS

For HCD

FOREWORD

Opera singing is an extreme sport. You know the sort of thing: jumping out of an aeroplane with a snowboard attached to your feet and no parachute, and expecting to land on – and glide effortlessly down – a mountainside in one piece. *It ain't gonna happen!* But the possibility that it might, and the thrill of attempting to attain that moment of glory, has kept me obsessed with this most thrilling of art forms all my life.

Opera lures you in with the magnificence of the music, the complexity of the characters and the thrilling spectacle – the design, the sets, the costumes, the lighting. Once the addiction takes hold, it's the unexpected things that happen which provide the greatest amusement. In my entire career, I have never been in an operatic production where something hasn't gone wrong at some point. Coping with these wonderful moments has given me some of my most joyous memories.

Take, for instance, Richard Jones's extraordinary 1992 production of *Die Fledermaus* for English National Opera, in which I played the role of Adele. I famously bared my all "for my art", but at the time that seemed as nothing compared with the other visual treats on offer. These included an electric cat, a real dog, an enormous carthorse (also very much alive) which pulled a spectacular *troika*. And as if that wasn't enough, we also had a gorilla (not real but very convincing). At one point on opening night, there was a strangled cry backstage from a much-harassed stage manager: "The dog is savaging the electric cat! For goodness sake, don't let the horse see the gorilla!"

On other occasions, I've been pinned to a table by a prematurely lowered chandelier, walked – and fallen off – a tightrope, and offered assistance with my breast pump. I've been locked out of cupboards I needed to get into, and locked into cupboards I needed to get out of, often with various inappropriate cast members (usually tenors). I've barely avoided landing in the orchestra pit when entering the stage full tilt on a bicycle, and I've stepped on a trapdoor that should have been locked and wasn't, disappearing under the stage mid-aria at Glyndebourne. (At which point, the tenor was very concerned as we had an imminent love scene, which was not scheduled to be sung underground!)

It's moments like these that embody the magic that opera holds for audience and singers alike. In the midst of glorious music, danger is never far away and laughter is always present. With all its myriad elements, every performance is – at the same time – a miracle, and a disaster, waiting to happen!

An Opera Miscellany captures something of the passion, as well as the hilarity and madness, to which I've devoted all of my adult life. Its author and I have shared our enthusiasm for opera over many years as we've worked on *The Opera Show* on

Classic FM radio. We've laughed uproariously more times than we can remember at the lunacy of the plots and the countless other extremities of operatic madness.

As for this book, well, it all started with a magic goat! Read on – and enjoy!

Lesley Garrett CBE

CURTAIN UP

Opera arouses very different responses in people. There are those who are so passionate about the art form that they spend their lives collecting, listening to and comparing recordings, booking their holidays around festivals and performances, and gossiping about its every aspect. And then there are those who simply can't stand it. Say the word "opera" and revulsion spreads across their faces, their minds filled with the stereotypical image of a hefty soprano, supposedly playing a consumptive teenager, managing to shriek at high pitch for several minutes while apparently dying. Opera is, after all, to quote Dr Johnson an "exotic and irrational entertainment".

Yet, between these two extremes are the football enthusiasts who have heard and loved Pavarotti singing 'Nessun Dorma', the promenade concert goers who've tapped their feet along with 'La donna è mobile', or the movie lovers whose breath was taken away by the use of a Mozart aria in *The Shawshank Redemption* or 'The Ride of the Valkyries' in *Apocalypse Now*.

If you count yourself among any of the above

categories of person, this book is for you. If you are a buff, I hope you will find in it some facts to impress your friends, or test the knowledge of your fellow enthusiasts. If you are an absolute beginner, then here's a potpourri – in no particular order – of the sublime and the ridiculous offering a taste of the many delights to be discovered.

Robert Weinberg

POETRY, MUSIC AND MACHINERY

As the British government consists of three estates: King, Lords and Commons, so an opera in its first institution consisted of Poetry, Music and Machinery.

Frances Burney

Opening bars

Legend has it that Wolfgang Amadeus Mozart wrote the overture to *Don Giovanni* (1787) on the morning of the opera's première, while suffering from a hangover. Realising the overture was still to be written, his wife Constanze plied him with punch on the night before the opera was scheduled to open, and read him stories to keep him alert while he began work on the overture. Eventually at three in the morning, Mozart begged Constanze to let him sleep for an hour. At 5 o'clock, she woke him up and Mozart set to work again. Two hours later, he delivered the overture, fully orchestrated, to the copyists.

Gioacchino Rossini was never too bothered about having an overture ready well in advance. "Wait till the evening of the day the opera is scheduled for performance," he laughed, "nothing excites the imagination more than necessity, the presence of a copyist waiting for the music, and the pressing of an impresario in despair tearing out his hair. In my day in Italy, all impresarios were bald by the age of thirty!"

Beethoven was the opposite to Rossini. For his only opera *Fidelio*, he tried out four different overtures. The first, for the opera's première in 1805, is thought to be the overture now performed in concert as 'Leonore No. 2'. A revised version of that is now known as 'Leonore No. 3'. This one was so powerful that it overwhelmed the opening scenes of the opera so Beethoven cut it back, creating 'Leonore No. 1'. For the 1814 revival of *Fidelio*, he started all over again and wrote what is now known as the *Fidelio* overture.

In the beginning – Old Testament characters at the opera

Adam, in *La mort d'Adam et son apothéose* by Jean-François Lesueur (1760–1837)

Cain and Abel, in *Abel* by Rodolphe Kreutzer (1766–1831)

Deborah, in *Dèbora e Jaéle* by Ildebrando Pizzetti (1880–1968)

Esther, in *Esther, princesse d'Israël* by Antoine Mariotte (1875–1944)

Jephtha, in *Jephté* by Michel Pignolet de Montéclair (1667–1737)

Job, in *Job* by Luigi Dallapiccola (1904–1975)

Joseph, in *La Légende de Joseph en Égypte* by Étienne Nicolas Méhul (1763–1817)

King David, in *David* by Darius Milhaud (1892–1974)

Moses, in *Mosè in Egitto* by Gioachino Rossini (1792–1868) and *Moses und Aron* by Arnold Schonberg (1874–1951)

Nebuchadnezzar, in *Nabucco* by Giuseppe Verdi (1813–1901)

Noah, in *Il diluvio universale* by Gateano Donizetti (1797–1848)

Ruth, in *Ruth* by Lennox Berkeley (1903–1989)

Samson and Delilah in *Samson et Dalila* by Camille Saint-Saëns (1835–1921)

Saul, in *Saul og David* by Carl Nielsen (1865–1931)

Opera etiquette

Pointers to help you have a great opera experience, suggested by Knoxville Opera.

(Reproduced from www.knoxvilleopera.com)

1. Please arrive on time. Be in your seat before the curtain goes up.
2. Please try not to talk during the performance. Wait until intermission or, if you must, whisper quietly.
3. Please do not sing or hum along with the performer. Instead, listen and watch everything carefully so you do not miss anything.
4. Please turn off all alarm watches, pagers, and cell phones. They can distract the performer as well as the audience.
5. Try to visit the restroom before the curtain goes up, or wait until intermission, so that you won't have to leave your seat during the performance.
6. You might wish to read the story of the opera before you see the performance.
7. Allow yourself to believe the story as it is told onstage. Suspension of disbelief is a powerful force!
8. Listen to the music and let your emotions respond.
9. Some people select their favorite character or singer and watch that performer carefully. You might look to identify what makes a particular artist stand out.
10. Enjoy yourself!

Five world premières conducted by Toscanini

1. *Pagliacci* by Ruggiero Leoncavallo – Milan, 21 May 1892
2. *La bohème* by Giacomo Puccini – Turin, 1 February 1896
3. *La Fanciulla del West* by Giacomo Puccini – New York, 10 December 1910
4. *Turandot* by Giacomo Puccini – Milan, 25 April 1926
5. *Il Re* by Umberto Giordano – Milan, 12 January 1929

Lost the Plot

The 40 most amazing opera plots

1. *Adriana Lecouvreur* (1902) by Francesco Cilea.
Paris, 1730. Michonnet, the director of the Comédie-Française is in love with one of his actresses Adriana Lecouvreur but doesn't tell her because she says she has a secret admirer. He discusses his dilemma with the theatre patron, the Prince de Bouillon. The Prince thinks his lover is having an affair with the Count of Saxony and the two are planning an assignation that night at her house. The Prince sets off to surprise the guilty pair. The letter is in fact from the Prince's wife not his lover, designed to catch her husband out. The Count was a former lover of hers. The Prince arrives and his wife hides, leaving the Count to deal with things. But then Adriana arrives. She hadn't realised the Count was her secret admirer. The Princess is fiercely jealous of Adriana and their rivalry escalates. A bunch of violets that Adriana had given to the Count – and that he had been compelled to present to the Princess – is returned to Adriana. But the Princess has put poison on the flowers that Adriana sniffs heartily. Just as the Count is declaring his true love to her, she drops dead – which really sort of spoils things.

Carmen collected

It's now the world's most popular opera, but Bizet's *Carmen* hasn't always charmed audiences or the critics. Its opening performances in 1875 were badly received and Bizet died before *Carmen*'s popularity soared.

> "In *Carmen* the composer has made up his mind to show us how learned he is, with the result that he is often dull and obscure."
> Léon Escudier (1816–81)

> "Take the Spanish airs and *mine* out of the score, and there remains nothing to Bizet's credit but the sauce that masks the fish."
> Charles Gounod (1818–93),
> on the première of *Carmen*

> "This music is wicked, refined, fatalistic: and withal remains popular – it possesses the refinement of a race, not of an individual."
> Friedrich Nietzsche (1844–1900)

> "It is difficult to think of an opera more suitable for a schoolboy."
> Sir Edward Heath (1916–2005)

> "They want manure – they can have it."
> Bizet on the 'Toreador Song'

(In a 1930s Covent Garden production, the audience got real manure courtesy of a horse, brought on stage in Act III. As the audience gasped, and the music stopped, the conductor Sir Thomas Beecham was heard to say, "A critic, by God".)

Lost the Plot

The 40 most amazing opera plots

2. *Alcina* (1735) by George Frideric Handel.
Bradamante and her companion arrive in the enchanted realm of Alcina, a sorceress who enslaves her male victims by turning them into particularly smelly flora and fauna. Bradamante wants to find her missing lover Ruggiero so she has disguised herself as her brother Ricciardo. Alcina's sister Morgana takes them to Ruggiero, who, bewitched, bewildered and bothered, has no recollection of his love for Bradamante. Alcina's general Oronte, who is in love with Morgana, becomes jealous when Morgana displays her attraction to Ricciardo – who is actually Bradamante. Ruggiero tries to convince Alcina to perform one of her transforming spells on Ricciardo. Morgana then declares her love for Ricciardo, or Bradamente, whichever way you want to look at it. Ruggiero is told the truth and is urged to run away. Ruggiero and Bradamante – no longer dressed as her brother thankfully – decide to defeat Alcina together. Alcina conjures spirits to stop Ruggiero from leaving, but they disobey her, and she finds her powers weakening. Alcina finds Ruggiero and forbids him to leave, but Ruggiero, deeply in love with Bradamante, refuses. Ruggiero recruits Oronte to his cause by offering him freedom. Alcina – who's losing her power – and her ugly sister plead for mercy, but Ruggiero destroys the source of the magic, vanquishing them both. Ding dong the witch is dead!

By Jupiter!

Ten operas in which the God Jupiter appears:

1. *La Calisto* (1651) by Francesco Cavalli (1602–76)
2. *Die Liebe der Danae* (1940) by Richard Strauss (1864–1949)
3. *Nais* (1745) by Jean-Philippe Rameau (1683–1764)
4. *The Olympians* (1949) by Sir Arthur Bliss (1891–1975)
5. *Orphée aux enfers* (1874) by Jacques Offenbach (1819–80)
6. *Il Paride* (1662) by Giovanni Andrea Bontempi (1625–1705)
7. *Philémon et Baucis* (1860) by Charles-François Gounod (1818–93)
8. *Platée* (1745) by Jean-Philippe Rameau (1683–1764)
9. *Il ritorno d'Ulisse in Patria* (1640) by Claudio Monteverdi (1567–1643)
10. *Semele* (1744) by George Frideric Handel (1685–1759)

The opera that sparked a riot

La muette de Portici –The mute girl of Portici – a five-act opera by Daniel Auber is one of the earliest of French grand operas. It tells the true story of a seventeenth century uprising in Naples against the occupying Spanish. For revolutionary Belgians, its big number 'Amour sacré de la patrie' became a new 'Marseillaise' and was sung everywhere.

After a performance at the Théâtre de la Monnaie, on 25 August 1830, during which the popular aria was sung by leading French tenor, Adolphe Nourrit (1802–39), the ignited audience poured out into the streets of Brussels, chanting patriotic slogans and rapidly taking possession of government buildings. The riot led to Belgium's independence from the Netherlands just five weeks later.

La muette de Portici is probably the only opera in which the eponymous heroine is non-singing – because she is mute, after all. In the nineteenth century, the role was often played by a leading ballerina.

All in the name

Opera singers throughout the centuries have adopted stage names to increase the aura of exoticism surrounding their lives and profession. Thus, American tenor Moses Adler became Norberto Ardelli. And German soprano Bertha Schwarz turned from black to white when she became Bianca Bianchi. Here are some more fantastic fabrications.

Charles Anthony . . . . Calogero Anthony Caruso
(American tenor)
Giuseppe Bentonelli . . . . Joseph Horace Benton
(American tenor)
Lucrezia Bori . . . . Lucrecia Borjas
(Spanish soprano)
Montserrat Caballe . . . . Maria de Montserrat
(Spanish soprano)   Viviana Concepción i Folc
José Carreras . . . . Josep Carreras i Coll
(Spanish tenor)
Mario Chamley . . . . Archer Ragland Cholmondeley
(American tenor)
Eleonora de Cisneros . . . . Eleanor Broadfoot
(American contralto)
Cristina Deutekom . . . . Stientje Engel
(Dutch soprano)
Placido Domingo . . . . José Plácido Domingo Embil
(Spanish tenor)
Farinelli . . . . Carlo Broschi
(Italian castrato)

Michael Langdon . . . . Frank Birtles
(British Bass)
Mario Lanza . . . . Alfredo Cocozza
(American tenor)
Jenny Lind . . . . Johanna Maria Lind
(Swedish soprano)
Lauritz Melchior . . . . Lebrecht Hommel
(Danish baritone)
Nellie Melba . . . . Helen Porter Mitchell
(Australian soprano)
Toti dal Monte . . . . Antonietta Meneghel
(Italian soprano)
Ernest Nicolini . . . . Ernest Nicholas
(French tenor)
Jan Peerce . . . . Jacob Pincus Perlemuth
(American tenor)
Ezio Pinza . . . . Ezio Fortunato
(Italian bass)
Lily Pons . . . . Alice Joséphine Pons
(French-born US soprano)
Rose Raisa . . . . Rose Burchstein
(Polish soprano)
Ernestine Schumann-Heink . . . . Tini Rössler
(German/Czech/Austrian contralto)
Elisabeth Schwarzkopf . . . . Olga Maria Elisabeth
(German-born Austrian/   Frederike Schwarzkopf
British soprano)
Senesino . . . . Francesco Bernardi
(Italian castrato)
Tito Schipa . . . . Raffaele Attilio Amadeo
(Italian tenor)

Beverly Sills . . . . Belle Miriam 'Bubbles' Silverman
(American soprano)

Giuseppina Strepponi . . . . Clela Maria Josepha Strepponi
(Italian soprano)

Renata Tebaldi . . . . Renata Ersilia Clotilde Tebaldi
(Italian soprano)

Richard Tucker . . . . Ruben Tickner
(American tenor)

Lost the Plot

The 40 most amazing opera plots

3. *Ariodante* (1735) by George Frideric Handel.
The Princess Ginevra is about to marry Ariodante, a vassal prince.
The Duke of Albany fancies her but she's rejected him. He asks her
lady-in-waiting Dalinda to help him get revenge. In the palace
garden, Ginevra and Ariodante prepare for their wedding. They
share their joy with shepherds and shepherdesses, as is often the case
in opera. The Duke persuades Dalinda to dress as Ginevra and to let
him in to the royal apartment. Later from the garden, Ariodante
sees Dalinda dressed as his beloved letting the Duke in. He thinks
she's being unfaithful and swears to kill himself. His brother
Lurcanio – who's in love with Dalinda – hatches another revenge
plot. News reaches Ginevra that Ariodante has drowned himself in
the sea. Lurcanio accuses Ginevra of betrayal. Ariodante – who isn't
dead but is rather wet – sees Dalinda being pursued by assassins sent
by the Duke. She tells him all about the plot and he vows to return.
The Duke convinces the King to let him marry Ginevra, against her
wishes. Ariodante bursts in. Lurcanio mortally wounds the Duke
who confesses the deception as he dies. Dalinda agrees to marry
Lurcanio and Ariodante marries Ginevra. And they all live happily
ever after, except the Duke who is dead.

Operatic Capriculture, or I'll get my goat

Goats, believe it or not, play an important role in several operas. The goat in Meyerbeer's *Dinorah* (1859) even has a name – Bellah. She is the pet of the leading lady who goes loopy when her house is hit by lightning and her betrothed – Hoël – leaves her to go in search of treasure, lured by the Wizard of Tonik. Delusional Dinorah sings Bellah a lullaby, 'Dors, petite, dors tranquille' (Sleep, little one, sleep peacefully) – perhaps the only example of a lullaby being sung to a goat in human history. Later in the opera, Bellah's bell is heard and the characters believe it will lead them to the treasure. They sing, 'Ce tintement que l'on entend' (That tinkling one hears). Act III opens with a duet for goatherds. By the end, Dinorah has been rescued and, with her sanity restored, she marries Hoël. Even Bellah joins the wedding procession as Goat of Honour!

In Gershwin's *Porgy and Bess* (1935), the paraplegic hero relies heavily on his goat-pulled cart to get him from A to B. At the end of the opera, Porgy determines to head off to New York City to recover Bess from the smooth-talking drug dealer Sportin' Life. "Fetch my goat!" Porgy yells triumphantly before the whole cast launches into 'O Lawd, I'm on my way!' There's no way a goat is going to last very long in New York's traffic.

An aria in Cilea's *L'Arlesiana*, 'Come due tizzi accesi' describes how a courageous goat puts up a fight against a hungry wolf that lasts all night. At daybreak, the exhausted goat collapses, as the sun kisses her and closes her eyes forever. Heartbreaking.

Other operas in which goats play a central role are *The Goat with the Golden Horns* (1921), considered to be the greatest achievement of Slovenian composer Viktor Parma; *Kemine and the Goat* (1945–46) by the Russian composer Adrian Grigor'yevich Shaposhnikov; *The Goat with Three Kids* (1939) by Alexandru Zirra; and *The Nanny Goat* (1897) also by Francesco Cilea, who obviously was a keen capriculturist.

Amongst the many vocal crimes committed by untrained or lesser singers of a certain age is a shaky trill known as the chevrotement – or "goat's trill". French singers were often the laughing stock of European operagoers for their tendency towards chevrotement.

Such a singer appears to have been on stage for the première of Donizetti's *L'Elisir d'Amore*. One critic described him as "a buffo with the voice of a goat."

Musicians with caprine names include the English contralto Clara Butt (1872–1936) and the Bohemia-born composer Samuel Capricornus (1628–65), whose numerous stage works are regrettably now lost.

The American Opera Company, founded in 1886, toured across the USA in the late nineteenth century with a chorus of 100 singers, an 80-strong ballet company, 25 principals, 500 pieces of scenery, 4000 costumes and, you guessed it, a live goat.

Lost the Plot

The 40 most amazing opera plots

4. *L'Arlesiana* (1897) by Francesco Cilea.
Down on a farm lives a widow, Rosa Mamai with her two sons –
Federico and l'Innocente who's a bit simple. Federico's got the hots
for a girl from Arles. Rosa sends her brother Marco off to gen up on
the unknown girl. He comes back with good but unreliable
information. But, all is spoilt by Metifio, a stable hand. He says he's
"been" with the girl from Arles and was dumped when her parents
thought she had better prospects with Federico. Federico runs off
distraught. L'Innocente discovers him hiding in a sheep pen. A
shepherd makes Federico an offer to take his mind off love. There's
nothing like working with sheep to help cope with rejection. Rosa's
god-daughter Vivetta tells Federico *she* loves him. Federico won't
marry the girl from Arles now and asks Vivetta to be his. Metifio
plans to abduct the girl and elope with her. Federico overhears and
is so overcome with jealousy he hits Metifio with a sledgehammer,
which is quite unpleasant. Federico sings a song about a goat
fighting all night with a wolf and falling dead at dawn. Federico's
obsessed with visions of the girl riding off. He heads for the barn to
get a look and falls to his death in the hay, which has to be the
last straw.

Ten operas based on works by Voltaire

The writings of Voltaire (1694–1778) have inspired some 60 operas. The author himself pops up as a character in Bernstein's *Candide*. Voltaire also wrote the libretti for a number of operas including *Samson* by Rameau.

1. *Alzira* (1845) by Verdi, inspired by *Alzire*
2. *Candide* (1958) by Bernstein, inspired by *Candide*
3. *Le Siège de Corinthe* (1826) by Rossini, inspired by *Mahomet*
4. *Statira* (1853) by Mercadante, inspired by *Olympie*
5. *Samson* (1732) by Rameau, inspired by *Samson*
6. *Semiramide* (1823) by Rossini, inspired by *Sémiramis*
7. *Tancredi* (1813) by Rossini, inspired by *Tancréde*
8. *Zaira* (1831) by Bellini, inspired by *Zaïre*
9. *La Belle Arséne* (1773) by Monsigny, inspired by *La Begueule*
10. *Isabelle et Gertrude* (1766) by Grétry, inspired by *Gertrude*

Seating capacity of some great opera houses

National Grand Theatre, Beijing
(under construction) 6500
Metropolitan Opera House, New York 3995
Civic Opera House, (Lyric Opera of Chicago) 3563
Dorothy Chandler Pavilion (Los Angeles Opera) ... 3197
Salle Wilfrid-Pelletier (Opéra de Montréal) 2982
Opera de la Bastille, Paris 2735
Detroit Opera House 2700
Southern Alberta Jubilee Auditorium, Calgary 2538
Brown Theatre (Houston Grand Opera) 2423
Edmonton Opera 2415
Hungarian National Opera 2400
Teatro Colón, Buenos Aires 2367
London Coliseum (English National Opera) 2358
The Opera Theatre, Seoul Arts Centre 2340
Kennedy Centre Opera House, Washington D.C. .. 2300
Royal Opera House, Covent Garden 2262
Ellie Caulkins Opera House, Denver 2225
Teatro alla Scala, Milan 2200
Teatro dell'Opera, Rome 2200
Großes Festspielhaus, Salzburg 2179
Santa Fe Opera House 2128
Four Seasons Centre for the Performing Arts,
Toronto 2000
Teatro Comunale, Florence 2000
Palacio de Bellas Artes, Mexico City 1977
Palais Garnier, Paris 1971

Wales Millennium Centre (Welsh National Opera) . . 1900
National Opera House, Oslo 1750
Vienna State Opera 1700
Harrison Opera House (Virginia Opera) 1632
Sydney Opera House 1507
Palace of Peace and Reconciliation, Astana,
Kazakhstan 1500
Copenhagen Opera House 1500
Vienna Volksoper 1473
Teatro Comunale Giuseppe Verdi, Trieste 1400
Finnish National Opera, Helsinki 1350
Gothenburg Opera 1301
Staatsoper, Berlin 1300
Glyndebourne 1242
Cairo Opera House 1200
Teatro Nacional de São Carlos, Lisbon 1148
Zurich Opera House 1100
Teatro Comunale, Bologna 1034
Drottningholms Slottsteater 900
Teatro Amazonas, Manaus 701
L'Opera de Monte-Carlo, Monaco 524

Get to Da Ponte, or ten amazing facts about Mozart's librettist

Lorenzo Da Ponte (1749–1838), the librettist for Mozart's *Le nozze di Figaro*, *Don Giovanni* and *Così fan tutte*:

1. Was born Jewish, but was ordained as a Catholic priest and trained as a teacher
2. Was banned from both professions for taking married women as mistresses
3. Claimed to have memorised most of Dante's *Inferno* in a six-month period
4. Was appointed poet to Italian opera at the King's Theatre London
5. Declared himself bankrupt to avoid going to debtor's prison
6. Also wrote the words for operas by Salieri, Paisiello and Soler
7. Ran a grocery store and gave Italian lessons in Philadelphia
8. Opened a bookstore in New York
9. Became first Professor of Italian Literature at Columbia College
10. Became a naturalised citizen of the USA at the age of 79

The Opera Hall of Shame

Of all the singers in history who genuinely believed they had some talent, Florence Foster Jenkins (1868–1944) was undoubtedly the worst. Jenkins inherited a large amount of money that allowed her to take up the singing career so actively discouraged by those who had heard her. Dubbed the "dire diva of din", she had no ability to pitch or sustain a note correctly and little rhythmic sense. Her appalling performances attracted an enormous fan following with Jenkins dismissing the laughter coming from the audience as "professional jealousy" from her rivals. After being involved in a taxi accident, when Jenkins found she could reach "a higher F than ever before", she sent cigars to the driver. A month before she died, Jenkins sold out Carnegie Hall.

Another soprano destined to remain in Opera's Hall of Shame is American socialite Tryphosa Bates-Batcheller (1876–1952). Her considerable wealth and social position enabled her to pursue her singing, appearing in many concerts, sometimes with the composer Massenet accompanying her. But, frankly, she was terrible.

Ten operas based on works by Schiller

The works of Friedrich Schiller (1759–1805) have inspired some 60 operas.

1. *Guillaume Tell* (1829) by Rossini, inspired by *Wilhelm Tell*
2. *I Masnadieri* (1847) by Verdi, inspired by *Die Räuber*
3. *Maria Stuarda* (1834) by Donizetti, inspired by *Maria Stuart*
4. *Luisa Miller* (1849) by Verdi, inspired by *Kabale und Liebe*
5. *Die Bürgschaft* (1816) by Schubert, inspired by *Die Bürgschaft*
6. *Don Carlos* (1866–84) by Verdi, inspired by *Don Carlos*
7. *Giovanna d'Arco* (1845) by Verdi, inspired by *Die Jungfrau von Orleans*
8. *La Chant de la Cloche* (1912) by d'Indy, inspired by *Das Lied von der Glocke*
9. *Fiesque* (1866) by Lalo, inspired by *Die Verschwörung des Fiesco zu Genua*
10. *Dimitrij* (1882–94) by Dvořák, inspired by *Demetrius*

Lost the Plot

The 40 most amazing opera plots

5. *Candide* **(1956) by Leonard Bernstein.**
Candide is the illegitimate nephew of a Baron and is in love with the Baron's daughter Cunégonde. But Candide is disliked by the Baron's son Maximilian. His professor, Pangloss instils in his students an undiluted optimism. The Baron thinks his nephew is socially inferior to his daughter and chucks him out. The Bulgar army attack and kill almost everyone including Cunégonde. Candide and his professor sail to Lisbon where they witness an earthquake and are arrested as heretics. The Professor is hanged and Candide is flogged. But, still hopeful, he travels on. In Paris, he recognises Cunégonde, who is alive after all. They flee to Cadiz where they are robbed and then decide to fight for the Jesuits in South America. In Buenos Aires, they bump into Maximilian who has also survived. Candide inadvertently stabs Maximilian and flees into the forest. He sails for Venice but his boat sinks. He is rescued by a raft on which he discovers Pangloss, still alive. In Venice, they meet Maximilian and Cunégonde again. They all attempt to console each other and buy a farm outside the city to start afresh. Here, our hero considers his optimism. He decides that life is really neither "good" nor "bad" but to be lived and made the best of.

From one to nine

A piece for:

One singer – aria
Two singers – duet
Three singers – trio
Four singers – quartet
Five singers – quintet
Six singers – sextet
Seven singers – septet
Eight singers – octet
Nine singers – nonet

Caruso on the San Fransisco earthquake

The great tenor Enrico Caruso was on tour in San Fransisco with the Metropolitan Opera company when the great 1906 earthquake struck, just hours after he had sung in *Carmen*. His account of the catastrophe appeared in London magazine, the *Sketch*:

"You ask me to say what I saw and what I did during the terrible days which witnessed the destruction of San Francisco? Well, there have been many accounts of my so-called adventures published in the American papers, and most of them have not been quite correct. Some of the papers said that I was terribly frightened, that I went half crazy with fear, that I dragged my valise out of the hotel into the square and sat upon it and wept; but all this is untrue. I was frightened, as many others were, but I did not lose my head. I was stopping at the [Palace] Hotel, where many of my fellow-artists were staying, and very comfortable it was. I had a room on the fifth floor, and on Tuesday evening, the night before the great catastrophe, I went to bed feeling very contented. I had sung in *Carmen* that night, and the opera had gone with fine *éclat*. We were all pleased, and, as I said before, I went to bed that night feeling happy and contented.

"But what an awakening! You must know that I am not a very heavy sleeper – I always wake early, and when I feel restless I get up and go for a walk. So on the Wednesday morning early I wake up about 5 o'clock, feeling my bed rocking as though I am in a ship on the ocean, and for a moment I think I am dreaming that I am crossing the water on my way to my beautiful country. And so I take no notice for the moment, and then, as the rocking continues, I get up and go to the window, raise the shade and look out. And what I see makes me tremble with fear. I see the buildings toppling over, big pieces of masonry falling, and from the street below I hear the cries and screams of men and women and children.

"I remain speechless, thinking I am in some dreadful nightmare, and for something like forty seconds I stand there, while the buildings fall and my room still rocks like a boat on the sea. And during that forty seconds I think of forty thousand different things. All that I have ever done in my life passes before me, and I remember trivial things and important things. I think of my first appearance in grand opera, and I feel nervous as to my reception, and again I think I am going through last night's *Carmen*.

"And then I gather my faculties together and call for my valet. He comes rushing in quite cool, and, without any tremor in his voice, says: 'It is nothing.' But all the same he advises me to dress quickly and go into the open, lest the hotel fall and crush us to powder. By this time the plaster on the ceiling has fallen in a great shower, covering the bed and the carpet and the furniture, and I, too, begin to think it is time to 'get busy'. My valet gives me some clothes; I know not what the garments are but I get into a pair of trousers and into a coat and draw some socks on and my shoes, and every now and again the room trembles, so that I jump and feel very nervous. I do not deny that I feel nervous, for I still think the building will fall to the ground and crush us. And all the time we hear the sound of crashing masonry and the cries of frightened people.

"Then we run down the stairs and into the street, and my valet, brave fellow that he is, goes back and bundles all my things into trunks and drags them down six flights of stairs and out into the open one by one. While he is gone for another and another, I watch those that have already arrived, and presently someone comes and tries to take my trunks saying they are his. I say, 'no, they are mine'; but he does not go away. Then a soldier comes up to me; I tell him that this man wants to take my trunks, and that I am Caruso, the artist who sang in *Carmen* the night before. He remembers me and makes the man who takes an interest in my baggage 'skiddoo' as Americans say.

"Then I make my way to Union Square, where I see some of my friends, and one of them tells me he has lost everything except his voice, but he is thankful that he has still got that. And they tell me to come to a house that is still standing; but I say houses are not safe, nothing is safe but the open square, and I prefer to remain in a place where there is no fear of being buried by falling buildings. So I lie down in the square for a little rest, while my valet goes and looks after the luggage, and soon I begin to see the flames and all the city seems to be on fire. All the day I wander about, and I tell my valet we must try and get away, but the soldiers will not let us pass. We can find no vehicle to find our luggage, and this night we are forced to sleep on the hard ground in the open. My limbs ache yet from so rough a bed.

"Then my valet succeeds in getting a man with a cart, who says he will take us to the Oakland Ferry for a certain sum, and we agree to his terms. We pile the luggage into the cart and climb in after it, and the man whips up his horse and we start.

"We pass terrible scenes on the way: buildings in ruins, and everywhere there seems to be smoke and dust. The driver seems in no hurry, which makes me impatient at times, for I am longing to return to New York, where I know I shall find a ship to take me to my beautiful Italy and my wife and my little boys.

"When we arrive at Oakland we find a train there which is just about to start, and the officials are very polite, take charge of my luggage, and tell me go get on board, which I am very glad to do. The trip to New York seems very long and tedious, and I sleep very little, for I can still feel the terrible rocking which made me sick. Even now I can only sleep an hour at a time, for the experience was a terrible one."

Twenty operas based on works by William Shakespeare

The plays of Shakespeare (1564–1614) have inspired some 300 operas. The writer even appears as a character in four operas, *Le Songe d'une Nuit d'Été* by Thomas, *La Gioventu di Shakespeare* by Lillo, *Guglielmo Shakespeare* by Benvenuti and *Shakespeare* by Serpette.

Ten most famous operas based on works by Shakespeare

1. *I Capuletti e I Montecchi* (1830) by Bellini, based on *Romeo and Juliet*
2. *Roméo et Juliette* (1867) by Gounod, based on *Romeo and Juliet*
3. *Otello* (1887) by Verdi, based on *Othello*
4. *Béatrice et Bénédict* (1862) by Berlioz, based on *Much Ado about Nothing*
5. *A Midsummer Night's Dream* (1960) by Britten, based on *A Midsummer Night's Dream*
6. *The Fairy Queen* (1692) by Purcell, based on *A Midsummer Night's Dream*
7. *Falstaff* (1893) by Verdi, based on *The Merry Wives of Windsor*
8. *Macbeth* (1847–65) by Verdi, based on *Macbeth*
9. *Antony and Cleopatra* (1974) by Samuel Barber, based on *Antony and Cleopatra*
10. *Otello* (1816) by Rossini, based on *Othello*

Ten lesser known operas based on works by Shakespeare

1. *Hermione* (1872) by Bruch, based on *A Winter's Tale*
2. *Der Widerspänstigen Zähmung* (1874) by Götz, based on *The Taming of the Shrew*
3. *Coriolanus* (1973) by Cikker, based on *Coriolanus*
4. *Imogène* (1796) by Kreutzer, based on *Cymbeline*
5. *Cordelia* (1881) by Gobatti, based on *King Lear*
6. *Das Liebesverbot* (1836) by Wagner, based on *Measure for Measure*
7. *Timone Misantropo* (1696) by Draghi, based on *Timon of Athens*
8. *Le Saphir* (1865) by David, based on *All's Well that Ends Well*
9. *Rosalinda* (1744) by Veracini, based on *As You Like It*
10. *At the Boar's Head* (1925) by Holst, based on *King Henry IV*

Singers on stamps

On 10 September 1997, the United States Postal Service issued four 32-cent commemorative postage stamps in the Legends of American Music series, celebrating opera singers. The singers featured were Lily Pons, Rosa Ponselle, Lawrence Tibbett and Richard Tucker.

Lost the Plot

The 40 most amazing opera plots

6. *Capriccio* (1942) by Richard Strauss.
A young, widowed Countess called Madeleine is about to celebrate her birthday. The composer Flamand and the poet Olivier both love her and argue about what'll impress her more – Flamand's music or Olivier's poetry? La Roche, who is another luvvie, says theatre is the greatest of all arts. He's directing a play starring the Countess's brother and an actress – Clairon – who's recently had an affair with Olivier. The Count teases his sister about her interest in Flamand. The Count fancies Clairon but doesn't believe in lasting love while the Countess longs for it. Clairon and the Count rehearse a scene from the play that ends with him reciting a passionate sonnet to her. Olivier tells the Countess he wrote the sonnet out of love for her. La Roche takes Olivier away to rehearse and Flamand declares *his* love to the Countess. He asks her to decide: music or poetry? Flamand or Olivier? As the arguments rage, the men all decide to combine their talents in an opera depicting the day's events. But how the opera will end is dependent on the Countess choosing which of the men she loves. After much indecision, soul-searching, navel-gazing and general prevarication, she realises that she's unable to make the choice that would give the opera an ending. So she goes to have dinner instead, which is a much better idea.

Sherlock Holmes at the opera

Sherlock Holmes enjoyed all sorts of music, including opera, and was a keen violinist. Having solved *The Adventure of the Red Circle,* Holmes and Watson rush to a Wagner night at Covent Garden. (In *The Red-Headed League,* Holmes tells Watson he prefers German music to French or Italian.)

In the story, *The Adventure of the Mazarin Stone,* Holmes fools his enemies into thinking he was playing the Barcarolle from Offenbach's *The Tales of Hoffman* on the violin, when he's actually playing them a gramophone recording.

Even the great Sherlock Holmes has been outwitted by a diva. Irene Adler in *A Scandal in Bohemia,* is a contralto who has performed at La Scala and at Warsaw's Imperial Opera. According to the story, the hereditary King of Bohemia visits Holmes and asks him to secure for him a photograph from Adler, his former lover, the existence of which would threaten his future marriage. Holmes manages to discover where the picture is hidden. When he goes to get it, he discovers Adler has vanished, along with her new husband and the picture, which has been replaced with a letter to the great detective.

Don Giovanni's conquests

The naughtiest boy in opera's women, as conveyed in the 'Catalogue Aria' by Don Giovanni's man-servant, Leporello:

In Italy, 640 women
In Germany, 231
In France, 100
In Turkey, 91
In Spain, 1001
Peasant girls,
Servants
Townspeople
Countesses
Baronesses
Marquesses
Princesses
Women of every class, shape and age
Blondes (he usually praises their manners)
Brunettes (their faithfulness)
Grey-haired ones (their sweetness)
Heavy ones (in winter)
Slim ones (in summer)
Big ones (majestic)
Little ones (charming)
Old ones (for the pleasure of adding them to the list)
Young beginners (his over-riding passion)
Rich, ugly or pretty (it doesn't matter so long as she has a skirt on)

Opera composers of Jewish origin

Leonard Bernstein (1918–90), composer of *Candide* and *A Quiet Place*

Aaron Copland (1900–90), composer of *The Tender Land* and *The Second Hurricane*

Paul Dukas (1865–1935), composer of *Ariane et Barbe-bleue*

George Gershwin (1898–1937), composer of *Blue Monday* and *Porgy and Bess*

Philip Glass (1937–), composer of *Akhnaten*, *Einstein on the Beach* and *Satyagraha*

Alexander Goehr (1932–), composer of *Arden Must Die*, *Behold the Sun* and *Arianna*

Osvaldo Golijov (1960–), composer of *Ainadamar*

Fromental Halévy (1799–1862), composer of *La Juive* and *L'eclair*

Erich Wolfgang Korngold (1897–1957), composer of *Die Tote Stadt* and *Violanta*

Giacomo Meyerbeer (1791–1864), composer of *Les Huguenots* and *Robert le Diable*

Darius Milhaud (1892–1974), composer of *Chrisophe Colomb* and *La mère coupable*

Jacques Offenbach (1819–1880), composer of *Orphée aux enfers*, *La Belle Hélène* and *Les Contes d'Hoffmann*

André Previn (1930–), composer of *A Streetcar named Desire*

Anton Rubinstein (1829–1894), composer of *The Demon* and *Die Maccabäer*

Arnold Schoenberg (1874–1951), composer of *Erwartung* and *Moses und Aron*

Franz Schreker (1878–1934), composer of *Der ferne Klang, Die Gezeichneten* and *Der Schatzgräber*

Kurt Weill (1900–50), composer of *Die Dreigroschenoper, Die Sieben todsünden,* and *Die Aufstieg und fall der stadt mahagonny*

Jaromír Weinberger (1896–1967), composer of *Svanda the Bagpiper*

Alexander von Zemlinsky (1871–1942), composer of *Sarema* and *Es war einmal*

Lost the Plot

The 40 most amazing opera plots

7. *Il Corsaro* (1848) by Giuseppe Verdi.
Corrado leads his pirates against the Muslims. Disguised as a
Dervish, he is taken to Pasha Seid and tells him he escaped from the
pirates and begs protection from his captors. When the day of the
attack comes, Corrado and his men reveal their true identity. He
rushes to the nearby harem to rescue its inhabitants. Among them
is Gulnara who falls in love with her saviour. The attack is crushed.
Corrado is captured and sentenced to death. Gulnara begs for his
life to be spared. Awaiting his painful end, Corrado worries about
Medora, the lover he has left behind. Gulnara reveals she loves him
and has prepared his escape. Corrado has resigned himself to his
fate and refuses to leave. Gulnara tries unsuccessfully to rally him so
goes off and kills Seid herself. Corrado agrees to leave only to spare
Gulnara her punishment for the crime. On the pirates' island,
Medora awaits Corrado's return. Certain of his death, she has
swallowed poison. A ship suddenly appears approaching the island
and is recognised as one of their own. Corrado arrives and relates
the tales of his journey to all. Medora thanks Gulnara for saving
Corrado and dies in his arms. In utter despair, Corrado jumps into
the sea as Gulnara faints.

Opera glass inflation

Opera glasses became a regular fixture in London theatres from the 1860s as patrons hired the small binoculars from attendants at the cost of one or two shillings for the performance.

At the beginning of the twentieth century, one Edward Ernest Morris of Covent Garden invented a coin-operated opera glass holder. In 1913, he founded the London Opera Glass Company and won contracts to place a sixpenny coin-operated holder in numerous theatres. New shilling-operated holders were introduced in 1968. Seven years later, following decimalization and the introduction of VAT, the 10p opera glass holder was developed. The new 20 pence coin led to the holders being adjusted again in 1982. In 1992, they were modified again to take two 20p pieces. The 50p model has been a familiar fixture in London theatres since 2000. According to the London Opera Glass Company's website (www.operaglasses.co.uk), the new tamper-proof holder "releases glasses near silently on insertion of single 50p coin".

Herring aids

Characters in Benjamin Britten's opera, *Albert Herring* (1947).

Lady Billows, *an elderly autocrat*
Florence Pike, *her housekeeper*
Miss Wordsworth, *a schoolteacher*
Mr. Gedge, *the vicar*
Mr. Upfold, *the mayor*
Superintendent Budd
Sid, *a butcher's assistant*
Albert Herring, *from the greengrocer's*
Nancy, *from the bakery*
Mrs. Herring, *Albert's mother*
Emmie
Cis
Harry

Recycling Rossini

Gioacchino Rossini was well into recycling long before bottle banks started appearing in his supermarket car park. The overture to *The Barber of Seville* had already been used for *Aureliano in Palmira* (1813) and *Elisabetta, regina d'Inghilterra* (1815). For *La Cenerentola* (1817), his version of the Cinderella story, he borrowed his own overture from an opera *La Gazzetta*, which had flopped the year before. In *La Gazzetta*, he had re-used tunes from *Il Turco in Italia* (1814) and *La pietra del paragone* (1812). The overture he wrote for *Il Turco in Italia* also found its way into *Sigismondo* (1814) and *Otello* (1816).

Partners in rhyme – ten operatic couples

1. **Giuseppe Verdi and Giuseppina Strepponi.** Verdi's affair with the soprano Strepponi began when the composer was 38. They lived together for twelve years before marrying in 1859. Strepponi starred in many of Verdi's early works including *Nabucco* and *Ernani*.

2. **Maria Spezia and Gottardo Aldighieri.** The 19th century Italian soprano triumphed as Violetta in *La Traviata* in Venice, and in *Nabucco* with her baritone husband who had carved a career for himself in grand opera in both Italy and England.

3. **Adelina Patti and Ernesto Nicolini.** Soprano Patti had been married for ten years to the Marquis de Caux, an Equerry to Napoleon III, when she began an affair with the tenor Nicolini in 1878. They set up home together at Craig-y-Nos, a large Victorian house in South Wales. They were married from 1886 until Nicolini's death in 1898.

4. **Clara Butt and Robert Kennerley Rumford.** The British contralto met her baritone husband in 1897, toured America with him, and married in Bristol Cathedral in 1900. So many people turned up for the wedding that the cathedral doors had to be locked, leaving thousands outside. After they married, Rumford would not allow his wife to take part in love scenes with other men so her operatic appearances more or less ended. The marriage lasted more than thirty years until her death.

5. **Dietrich Fischer-Dieskau and Julia Varady.** The Romanian soprano married the German baritone in 1978. "He has been the central encounter in my professional life," she said. "My husband was always a mirror who made my strengths and weaknesses apparent to me, and even his criticism was kind and productive... Above all he has always complained that my German isn't yet perfect."

6. **Richard Strauss and Pauline de Ahna.** Richard Strauss was conducting at Weimar where Pauline de Ahna was a soprano. By all accounts, Pauline was a nightmare, who often critically panned his work. Strauss told Mahler, "She gets horribly angry a lot, but that's what I need."

7. **Benjamin Britten and Peter Pears.** Britten and Pears met in 1936 and became lifelong partners. Much of Britten's music contains taxing tenor roles written for Pears, notably *Peter Grimes*, *Albert Herring*, Captain Vere in *Billy Budd*, Aschenbach in *Death in Venice* and Quint in *The Turn of the Screw*.

8. **Dame Joan Sutherland and Richard Bonynge.** Working as an accompanist, Richard Bonynge became a coach for Joan Sutherland in London although he had accompanied her previously in their native Australia. They married in 1954. It was Bonynge who convinced her to concentrate on the *bel canto* repertoire, turning her into an operatic superstar. From 1962 onwards, Bonynge conducted most of Dame Joan's performances. With his expertise and appreciation of her voice and the

operatic repertoire, her career was meticulously
planned out.

9. **Mirella Freni and Nikolai Ghiaurov.** Freni, one of
the world's favourite post-war Italian sopranos, was
married for many years to the Bulgarian bass
Ghiaurov. "He can help me, just as I can help him.
We try to appease each other with love and
humanity," she told *Time* magazine in 1981.

10. **Roberto Alagna and Angela Gheorghiu.** Alagna's first
wife died of a brain tumour in 1994. In 1996, he
married Angela Gheorghiu with whom he has
performed often on stage and on record. They also
starred in a 2001 film version of *Tosca*.

Lost the Plot

The 40 most amazing opera plots

8. *La fille du régiment* (1840) by Gaetano Donizetti.
Victorious Napoleonic troops are marching on a Tyrolean village.
With them is Marie, who was found on the battlefield as a child –
which was a strange place to be playing – and was raised by the
entire company. She is unhappy because she's in love with a young
man – Tonio, who saved her life. But she may only marry a
grenadier. The soldiers find Tonio hiding and want to kill him
because they think he's a spy but Marie pleads for him. They sign
Tonio up to the regiment and say he can marry Marie. A local
Marchioness asks for safe conduct back to Berkenfeld. She's asked if
she has known a Robert Berkenfeld since Marie's papers have that
name on them. The Marchioness says that Marie is her niece and
must live with her. She arranges for Marie to marry the son of the
duchess of Crackentorp. Marie would rather be with Tonio who
tells the Marchioness of his love for Marie. Tonio also reveals that
he's discovered that the Marchioness had no siblings so Marie could
not be her niece and is free to marry anyone she chooses. The
Marchioness confesses that she's actually Marie's mother. Tonio and
the rest of the company burst in to Marie's wedding to Crackentorp
and Marie tells all how she considers the entire regiment to be her
fathers, which must be problematic buying gifts when Father's Day
comes around. The Marchioness is so moved she allows Marie to
marry Tonio.

It's murder out there

In the spring of 1840, real life drama spilled over onto the stage of the opera house in Lucca. Two of the performers in a production of Donizetti's *Lucia di Lammermoor* had been feuding but were reconciled after fighting a duel. During the second act of the opera, however, memories of their former animosity re-emerged as their on-stage fight turned into a genuine one. The audience went wild, cheering the passion and drama of the acting. Suddenly, however, the singer playing Ravenswood let out a spine-tingling scream as his opponent's sword went straight into his chest, killing him. The other singer was arrested and the production was shut down the next day.

In 1922, the French tenor Louis Cazette was injured by a trident being carried in a rehearsal of Gounod's opera *Mireille,* by the baritone André Baugé. Tetanus infection set in and he died soon afterwards at the age of 34.

The German soprano Gertrud Bindernagel died at the age of 38, after being shot by her second husband. As she was walking through the opera arcade following a performance of *Siegfried* in Berlin, he opened fire on her. At his trial, it emerged that he had imagined his wife and her lover were conspiring against him. There was, in fact, no plot and no lover.

The sweet smell of excess –
Rossini's dietary habits

In Rossini's *La Cenerentola*, Don Magnifico anticipates the culinary delights that the marriage of his daughter to the Prince will bring:

"Sarò zeppo e contornato di memorie e petizioni, di galline e di storioni, di bottiglie di broccati, di candele e marinati, di ciambelle e pasticcetti, di canditi e di confetti, di piastroni, di dobloni, di vaniglia e di caffè." (I will have lots of memories and petitions, of hens and sturgeons, of bottles and brocades, of candles and marinades, of buns and cakes, of candied fruits and sweets, of slaps and doubloons, of vanilla and coffee.)

Such a list would have represented a commonplace meal for Rossini whose appetite for food and drink was legendary. It's said that his taste for wine was cultivated when he served as an altar boy. The aria, 'Di tanti palpiti' from *Tancredi* became known as the 'rice aria' when a rumour spread that Rossini wrote it while waiting for risotto in a Venice restaurant. Rossini is said to have burst into tears on one occasion when a picnic basket containing his favourite dish – turkey stuffed with truffles – went overboard during a boating outing. It's also reported that on the night of the première of *The Barber of Seville*, Rossini rushed through the performance to immerse himself in a lengthy description of an exotic salad recipe which became known as an *Ensalada alla Rossini*. Other dishes that Rossini inspired included: *Tournedos Rossini* – a rich concoction of tenderloin steak, *foie gras*, truffles and madiera sauce; small *Pasticcini* cakes inspired by Figaro; and an apple pie served to celebrate the completion of *William Tell*, decorated with a sugar apple complete with arrow. Today, in the Greek port of Salonika, you can enjoy Soup *alla Rossini*, made of mashed vegetables with dill; *Cannelloni alla Rossini* is a favourite in Spain and in Argentina; in Los Angeles, try the Fillet of Sole *alla Rossini*; at Raffles in Singapore, relish the *Pheasant Suprême alla Rossini;* and *Rossini Pizza* with eggs and mayonnaise, created in Pesaro, has reached California with seven different toppings.

All the best tunes

Operas in which the devil appears:

Angelique (1927) by Jacques Ibert
Cherivichki (1885) by Pyotr Il'yich Tchaikovsky
Christmas Eve (1895) by Nikolay Rimsky-Korsakov
The Damnation of Faust (1846) by Hector Berlioz
The Devil and Daniel Webster (1939) by Douglas S. Moore
The Devil and Kate (1899) by Antonín Dvorák
The Devil take Her (1931) by Arthur Benjamin
Doktor Faust (1787) by Ignaz Walter
Doktor Faust (1925) by Ferruccio Busoni
Faust (1816) by Louis Spohr
Faust (1859) by Charles Gounod
The Fiery Angel (1907) by Sergey Prokofiev
Grisélidis (1891) by Jules Massenet
Hry o Marii (1935) by Bohuslav Martinu
Irische Legend (1951–55) by Werner Egk
Mefistofele (1868) by Arrigo Boito
Robert le diable (1831) by Giacomo Meyerbeer
Schwanda the Bagpiper (1927) by Jaromír Weinberger

Lost the Plot

The 40 most amazing opera plots

9. *L'Elisir d'Amore* (1832) by Gaetano Donizetti.
A young villager Nemorino is in love with the fickle, farm owner Adina. She tells him his time would be better spent looking after his ailing uncle than trying to woo her. Sergeant Belcore swaggers in and asks Adina to marry him. A dodgy travelling salesman Dr. Dulcamara arrives in the town and Nemorino asks him if he sells a love potion. Dulcamara gives the boy a bottle of wine and takes his last penny. Nemorino gets very drunk. Snubbing him in his sozzled state, Adina agrees to marry Belcore. Nemorino begs her to wait another day. She refuses. At the pre-wedding feast, Nemorino arrives and begs Dulcamara for another bottle of potion. In order to get some money to buy it, Nemorino signs up to the army under Belcore. Even drunker than before, Nemorino learns that his uncle has just died and left him a small fortune. Adina sees him leave with a bevy of beauties. She's furious that he has sold his freedom to Belcore. Adina decides to woo Nemorino. She buys back his enlistment papers and tells him she loves him. Back in the piazza, Belcore marches in to find Adina now attached to Nemorino. Belcore slinks off, saying thousands of women await him elsewhere. Dulcamara attributes Nemorino's happiness and inheritance to the potion and quickly sells more bottles before making his escape.

Lullistes v Ramistes

Long before the mods and rockers battled it out on Brighton beach, eighteenth-century French composers inspired similar degrees of adoration and violence between their fans. The great French composer, Jean-Philippe Rameau (1683–1764) did not write his first opera until he was 50. *Hippolyte et Aricie* (1733) brought a new dramatic intensity to opera and was acclaimed by many as bold and daring, but dismissed by others as "turbulent" and "a lot of noise". Fans of the late Jean-Baptiste Lully (1632–87) were outraged. They were worried that Rameau's growing popularity would push Lully's music out of the repertoire. The *Lullistes* attacked Rameau's operas while *Ramistes* hailed their hero as the "new Orpheus". Tension grew between the two factions throughout the 1730s. When Rameau's opera *Dardanus* opened in 1739, the composer became the subject of satirical engravings and a poem that led to fisticuffs with Lully's librettist Charles-Pierre Roy, who had sided with the conservatives. The *Ramistes* bought as many tickets for *Dardanus* as they could to pack out the audience. But its first run of 26 performances was not the success the composer and his fans had hoped for.

What's Opera Doc?

Operatic excesses have fed the imagination of Hollywood's greatest animators, with *The Barber of Seville* and the sextet from *Lucia di Lammermoor* popping up most frequently in cartoon classics. Bugs Bunny's first foray into opera was *Long-Haired Hare* (1949) which features the *Barber* aria "Largo al factotum". The following year, *The Rabbit of Seville* (1950) sees Bugs playing the barber, tormenting the hirsutically challenged Elmer Fudd. Woody Woodpecker also tried his hand at opera and hair-dressing in *The Barber of Seville* (1944). In *Notes to You* (1941), Porky Pig is kept awake at night by an alley cat howling 'Largo al factotum'. After Porky shoots the cat, a chorus of ghostly felines arrives to sing the *Lucia* sextet. The cartoon was remade in 1948 with Elmer Fudd and Sylvester. Tex Avery's *The Magical Maestro* (1952) tells the story of a man trying to sing *The Barber of Seville* as a magician persists in transforming his costumes. In Disney's *The whale who wanted to sing at the Met* (1946), Nelson Eddy voiced Willie the whale who can sing tenor, baritone and bass at the same time. Willie dreams of auditioning with 'Largo al factotum' and the *Lucia* sextet before singing *Pagliacci* at the Met, with the "motley" on, his whale tears requiring the audience to put up umbrellas.

The Disney studio also brought the ultimate diva to cinema screens – Clara Cluck, a full-bodied and not particularly talented chicken, voiced by singer Florence Gill. Clara Cluck sang Juliet to Donald Duck's Romeo in

Mickey's Grand Opera (1934) and gobbled her way singlehandedly through the *Lucia* sextet in *The Orphans' Benefit* (1934).

Animation's finest opera moment by far was *What's Opera, Doc?* (1957) in which Wagner's *Ring* is compressed into just six minutes. Elmer Fudd in armour chases Bugs Bunny across mountains intoning "Kill da wabbit, kill da wabbit" to the tune of the 'Ride of the Valkyries'. Even Pablo Picasso is said to have admired the artistry of *What's Opera, Doc?*

Other cartoon characters encountering opera included Mr Magoo, stumbling his way chaotically through an opera in *Stage Door Magoo* (1955), magpies Heckle and Jeckle in *Off to the Opera* (1952), and Gandy Goose in *Carmen's Veranda* (1944).

The 20 greatest sopranos of all time

In April 2007, *BBC Music* magazine asked a panel of opera critics, academics, radio producers and presenters to draw up their ultimate list of great sopranos.

1. Maria Callas (1923–77)
2. Joan Sutherland (1926–)
3. Victoria de los Angeles (1923–2005)
4. Leontyne Price (1927–)
5. Birgit Nilsson (1918–2005)
6. Montserrat Caballé (1933–)
7. Lucia Popp (1939–93)
8. Margaret Price (1941–)
9. Kirsten Flagstad (1895–1962)
10. Emma Kirkby (1949–)
11. Elisabeth Schwarzkopf (1915–2006)
12. Régine Crespin (1927–)
13. Galina Vishnevskaya (1926–)
14. Gundula Janowitz (1937–)
15. Karita Mattila (1960–)
16. Elisabeth Schumann (1888–1952)
17. Christine Brewer (1960–)
18. Renata Tebaldi (1922–2004)
19. Rosa Ponselle (1897–1981)
20. Elly Ameling (1933–)

Showing his own trumpet

For *Aida*, Giuseppe Verdi envisaged a particular kind of extra-long trumpet for the Triumph Scene, which did not exist. So he had it made especially.

The trumpet was manufactured in France and was also called *trompette thébaine* or "trumpet of Thebes". It produced only four notes A flat, B flat, B natural and C.

The score of Aida requires six of them.

Lost the Plot

The 40 most amazing opera plots

10. *L'Étoile* (1877) by Emmanuel Chabrier.
The neurotic and insecure King Ouf I entertains his subjects annually on his birthday with a public execution. This year his choice of victim is a handsome peddler called Lazuli who accidentally struck the King without knowing who he was. However, King Ouf's astrologer Siroco tells the King that his star sign and that of Lazuli are so intimately bound up that they will both die on the same day. The terrified King cancels the execution and lavishes his favours all over Lazuli. Nothing is too good for the man who the King has to keep alive at all costs. In the meantime, a pompous foreign Ambassador arrives on the scene. His name is Herisson de Porc-Epic. He's determined to marry off his daughter Laoula to King Ouf. Porc-Epic is also having trouble with his attractive but unfaithful wife and his secretary Tapioca. It all gets very confusing. Just as everything is about to fall apart, Siroco the astrologer returns and sorts all their shenanigans out. The bemused peddler Lazuli even wins the love of the Princess Laoula. Not bad for someone who was about to be put to death.

Crazy but true – real life characters in opera

Jack the Ripper. The Victorian serial killer pops up at the end of Alban Berg's *Lulu* (1937), murdering the eponymous heroine and her admirer, the Countess Geschwitz.

The Elephant Man. The horribly deformed nineteenth-century society celebrity is the subject of Laurent Petitgirard's opera, *Joseph Merrick de Elephant Man* (2002).

Diana, Princess of Wales. The Nuremberg Opera production, *A Lady Dies*, staged in 2000, told the Princess's story using the device of three royalists – an elderly woman, a hairdresser and her niece. Music was by Stefan Hippe, libretto by Gerhard Falkner.

Albert Einstein. Philip Glass's first theatre piece *Einstein on the Beach* (1976) runs five hours with no intermission. Glass has also been inspired by Galileo in *Galileo Galilei* (2002), Christopher Columbus and Stephen Hawking in *The Voyage* (1992), and Egyptian pharaoh, *Akhanaten* (1984).

Marco Polo. Tan Dun incorporated shadow theatre, kabuki and Peking opera into his opera, *Marco Polo* (1995).

Sayings of Otis B. Driftwood

Aka Groucho Marx in *A Night at the Opera,* (1935):

"You're willing to pay him a thousand dollars a night just for singing? Why, you can get a phonograph record of Minnie the Moocher for 75 cents. And for a buck and a quarter, you can get Minnie."

"Was that a high C, or Vitamin D?"

"And now, on with the opera. Let joy be unconfined. Let there be dancing in the streets, drinking in the saloons, and necking in the parlour."

To carriage driver: "Hey you. I told you to slow that nag down. On account of you I almost heard the opera."

"I am sure the familiar strains of Verdi's music will come back to you tonight, and Mrs. Claypool's cheques will probably come back to her in the morning."

"Signor Lassparri comes from a very famous family. His mother was a well-known bass singer. His father was the first man to stuff spaghetti with bicarbonate of soda, thus causing and curing indigestion at the same time."

Driftwood: "You see that spaghetti? Now, behind that spaghetti is none other than Herman Gottlieb, director of the New York Opera Company. Do you follow me?"

Mrs. Claypool: "Yes."

Driftwood: "Well stop following me or I'll have you arrested!"

Le roi s'amuse

The concept of "royal God-given rights" seems to extend, for some monarchs at least, to passing judgement on opera. Most famously, Emperor Joseph II advised Mozart after the 1782 première of *Die Entführung aus dem Serail,* "Very many notes, my dear Mozart," to which the composer replied "Exactly the necessary number, your Majesty."

In 1860, Queen Victoria told her eldest daughter Vicky in a letter, "Mozart I am not always quite so fond of, as I think the instrumentation so poor (it was so those days) … Some of Bellini's are lovely – (Papa even likes many of them). *Rigoletto* too, has some very pretty things, but not the *Traviata* or *Ernani*."

Richard Strauss came in for some stick from two royals. Kaiser Wilhelm II remarked, "I really like this fellow Strauss but *Salome* will do him a lot of damage". The Kaiser's cousin, King George V was less gracious. After the band of the Grenadier Guards had played a selection of themes from Richard Strauss's *Elektra* in the courtyard of Buckingham Palace, the director of music was informed, "His Majesty does not know what the Band has just played but it is *never* to be played again."

While attending operas at Covent Garden, Queen Victoria was not amused by the blue lights of Bow Street Police Station across the road. It became the only police station in London not to have blue lights outside.

Lost the Plot

The 40 most amazing opera plots

11. *Faust* (1859) by Charles Gounod.
This is the story of a morose and pessimistic man. Just as Faust is about to end it all, the devil appears and tells him he should go out and experience the world rather than sitting around moping. The devil lures him to sleep by the banks of the river where he's given seductive dreams of a pretty girl. On waking, Faust demands to be taken to her. The girl – Marguerite – has seen him already, also in a dream. They meet and declare their love for one another. But the devil interrupts and urges Faust to flee as the curtain-twitching neighbours have gone to warn Marguerite's mother. Faust jilts Marguerite and goes off to renew his strength in the midst of nature. The devil arrives and tells him that Marguerite is in prison awaiting execution for killing her mother, a crime for which Faust is responsible! The devil is prepared to rescue her on condition that Faust seals their pact with his signature. It's a trap and Faust is led off into the depths of hell amidst thunder and bloody rain. Faust is thrown into the flames for an eternal barbecue, while Marguerite is welcomed into heaven.

Coming to America

Operas featuring Christopher Columbus:

Cristoforo Colombo (1892) by Alberto Franchetti
Christophe Colomb (1930) by Darius Milhaud
Christopher Columbus (first perf. 1976) by
    Jacques Offenbach
The Voyage (1992) by Philip Glass

All that glitters

Probably the most expensive opera costume of all time was worn by Adelina Patti (1843–1919), one of the giants of nineteenth-century opera, acclaimed by Verdi as the greatest singer he had ever heard. Appearing as Violetta in *La Traviata* at Covent Garden in 1895, Patti wore a white dress encrusted with 3700 diamonds. The jewels were estimated to be worth £200,000 (more than £15 million at today's prices). Not surprisingly, two officers from Bow Street police station across the road from the opera house appeared on stage among the "guests" in the party scene.

Cleopatra, coming at ya

The life and loves of Cleopatra, Queen of Egypt (69–30 BC) have inspired at least 50 operas, with Shakespeare's play, *Antony and Cleopatra* being a major influence on composers.

The first composer to write a Cleopatra opera appears to have been Antonio Canazzi in 1653. Towards the end of the eighteenth century, there was a plethora of Cleopatra stories on the opera stage including works by Monza, Anfossi, Cimarosa, Nasolini, Guglielmi, Weigl and Paer. Rossi and Morales wrote Italian versions in the late nineteenth century. Bondeville's *Antoine et Cléopâtre* and Massenet's *Cléopâtre* are among the more successful French offerings.

The first German version was Mattheson's *Die unglückselige Cleopatra, Königin von Egypten* in 1704. Other German composers who have fallen for the charms of the Egyptian queen include Danzi, Sulzer, Hasse, Graun and Goldberg. Handel featured her in *Giulio Cesare*. American composers inspired by the story are Hadley in *Cleopatra's Night* (1920) and Barber's *Antony and Cleopatra* (1966). Nearly all of the Cleopatra operas end with her death by asp bite.

Lost the Plot

The 40 most amazing opera plots

12. *La Forza del Destino* (1862) by Giuseppe Verdi.
Leonora's father has separated her from her suitor Don Alvaro and
the couple plan to elope. As they are about to set off, the father
returns and orders Alvaro's arrest. Alvaro's pistol accidentally
explodes and kills the father who curses Leonora as she leaves. Her
brother Don Carlo pursues his sister who has now taken to dressing
as a man. A monk lets her use a hermit's cave near to the monastery.
Alvaro, who thinks Leonora is dead, joins the army and saves Carlo
– also a soldier – from an attempted assassination. The two men
become great pals and hug each other a lot. But when Alvaro is
injured, Carlo discovers Alvaro is the killer of his father. He
challenges him to a duel but Alvaro refuses and decides to join the
monastery that is sheltering Leonora (although he doesn't know it).
Don Carlo pursues him and they have a scrap. Carlo is mortally
wounded. Alvaro enters the cave and asks the hermit – who is
Leonora – to come and help. They all recognise each other and
Carlo strikes his sister a mortal blow. She tells Alvaro that she is
looking forward to a reunion in heaven with him while he curses
the forces that govern their destiny.

Opera composers and their essential works

Adolphe Adam (1803–56): *Le postillon de Lonjumeau*
John Adams (1947–): *The Death of Klinghoffer, Nixon
in China*
Thomas Adès (1971–): *Powder Her Face, The Tempest*
Isaac Albéniz (1860–1909): *Pepita Jiménez*
Daniel-François-Esprit Auber (1782–1871): *Fra Diavolo,
La muette de Portici*
Michael Balfe (1808–70): *The Bohemian Girl*
Samuel Barber (1910–81): *Antony and Cleopatra, Vanessa*
Béla Bartók (1881–1945): *Bluebeard's Castle*
Ludwig van Beethoven (1770–1827): *Fidelio*
Vincenzo Bellini (1801–35): *Beatrice di Tenda, I Capuleti
e i Montecchi, Norma, Il pirata, I puritani,
La sonnambula*
Richard Rodney Bennett (1936–): *The Mines of Sulphur*
Alban Berg (1885–1935): *Lulu, Wozzeck*
Luciano Berio (1925–2003): *Un re in ascolto*
Hector Berlioz (1803–69): *Béatrice et Bénédict, Benvenuto
Cellini, The Damnation of Faust, Les Troyens*
Leonard Bernstein (1918–90): *Candide*
Harrison Birtwistle (1934–): *Gawain, The Mask of Orpheus*
Georges Bizet (1835–75): *Carmen, La jolie fille de Perth,
The Pearl Fishers*
John Blow (1649–1708): *Venus and Adonis*
François-Adrien Boïeldieu (1775–1834): *La dame blanche*
Arrigo Boito (1842–1918): *Mefistofele*
Alexander Borodin (1833–87): *Prince Igor* (Knyaz Igor)

Rutland Boughton (1878–1960): *The Immortal Hour*
Benjamin Britten (1913–76): *Albert Herring, Billy Budd, Death in Venice, Gloriana, A Midsummer Night's Dream, Owen Wingrave, Peter Grimes, The Rape of Lucretia, The Turn of the Screw*
Ferruccio Busoni (1866–1924): *Doktor Faust*
Alfredo Catalani (1854–93): *La Wally*
Francesco Cavalli (1602–76): *Calisto*
Emmanuel Chabrier (1841–94): *L'étoile, Le roi malgré lui*
Gustave Charpentier (1860–1956): *Louise*
Marc-Antoine Charpentier (1643–1704): *Médée*
Ernest Chausson (1855–99): *Le roi Arthus*
Luigi Cherubini (1760–1842): *Médée*
Francesco Cilea (1866–1950): *Adriana Lecouvreur, L'arlesiana*
Domenico Cimarosa (1749–1801): *Il matrimonio segreto*
Aaron Copland (1900–90): *The Tender Land*
Peter Maxwell Davies (1934–): *The Lighthouse, Taverner*
Claude Debussy (1882–1918): *Pelléas et Mélisande*
Léo Delibes (1836–91): *Lakmé*
Frederick Delius (1862–1934): *Koanga, A Village Romeo and Juliet*
Gaetano Donizetti (1797–1848): *Anna Bolena, L'assedio di Calais, Il castello di Kenilworth, Don Pasquale, L'elisir d'amore, Emilia di Liverpool, La favorite, La fille du régiment, Lucia di Lammermoor, Lucrezia Borgia, Maria Stuarda, Poliuto, Roberto Devereux, Rosmonda d'Inghilterra*
Paul Dukas (1865–1935): *Ariane et Barbe–Bleue*
Antonín Dvořák (1841–1904): *Dimitrij, The Jacobin, Rusalka*

Manuel de Falla (1876–1946): *La vida breve*

Gabriel Fauré (1845–1924): *Pénélope, Prométhée*

Carlisle Floyd (1926–): *Susannah*

Edward German (1862–1936): *Merrie England*

George Gershwin (1898–1937): *Porgy and Bess*

Umberto Giordano (1867–1948): *Andrea Chénier, Fedora*

Philip Glass (1937–): *Akhnaten, Einstein on the Beach, Satyagraha*

Mikhail Glinka (1804–57): *A Life for the Tsar, Ruslan and Lyudmila*

Christoph Willibald Gluck (1714–87): *Alceste, Armide, Orfeo ed Euridice*

Benjamin Godard (1849–95): *Jocelyn*

Charles Gounod (1818–93): *Faust, Roméo et Juliette*

Fromental Halévy (1799–1862): *La Juive*

George Frideric Handel (1685–1759): *Acis and Galatea, Agrippina, Alcina, Almira, Ariodante, Giulio Cesare, Hercules, Orlando, Ottone, Radamisto, Rinaldo, Rodelinda, Samson, Semele, Serse, Teseo*

Joseph Haydn (1732–1809): *Armida, Il mondo della luna, Orlando paladino, La vera costanza*

Hans Werner Henze (1926–): *Boulevard Solitude, Elegy for Young Lovers, We Come to the River, The Bassarids*

Louis Joseph Ferdinand Herold (1791–1833): *Zampa*

Gustav Holst (1874–1934): *The Perfect Fool, Savitri*

Arthur Honegger (1892–1955): *Jeanne d'Arc au bûcher*

Engelbert Humperdinck (1854–1921): *Hänsel und Gretel*

Leos Janácek (1854–1928): *The Cunning Little Vixen, Destiny, From the House of the Dead, Jenufa, Kátya Kabanová, The Makropulos Affair*

Scott Joplin (1867–1917): *Treemonisha*

Zoltán Kodály (1882–1967): *Háry János*
Erich Wolfgang Korngold (1897–1957): *Die tote Stadt*
Édouard Lalo (1823–1892): *Le roi d'Ys*
Franz Lehár (1870–1948): *Der Graf von Luxemburg, The Land of Smiles, The Merry Widow (Die lustige Witwe), Paganini, Der Zarewitsch*
Ruggiero Leoncavallo (1857–1919): *Pagliacci*
György Ligeti (1923–2006): *Le Grand Macabre*
Jean-Baptiste Lully (1632–87): *Acis et Galatée, Armide, Atys*
Bohuslav Martinu (1890–1958): *The Greek Passion, Julietta*
Pietro Mascagni (1863–1945): *L'amico Fritz, Cavalleria rusticana, Iris*
Jules Massenet (1842–1912*)*: *Le Cid, Don Quichotte, Esclarmonde, Hérodiade, Manon, Thaïs, Werther*
Gian-Carlo Menotti (1911–2007): *Amahl and the Night Visitors, The Consul, The Medium, The Saint of Bleeker Street*
Olivier Messiaen (1908–1992): *Saint François d'Assise*
Giacomo Meyerbeer (1791–1864): *L'Africaine, Il crociato in Egitto, L'esule di Granata, Margherita d'Anjou, Le prophète, Robert le diable*
Claudio Monteverdi (1567–1643): *L'incoronazione di Poppea, Orfeo, Il ritorno d'Ulisse in patria*
Wolfgang Amadeus Mozart (1756–91): *La clemenza di Tito, Così fan tutte, Don Giovanni, Die Entführung aus dem Serail, Idomeneo, The Magic Flute, The Marriage of Figaro, Mitridate, re di Ponto, Zaide*
Modest Mussorgsky (1839–81): *Boris Godunov, Khovanshchina, Salammbô*

Carl Otto Nicolai (1810–49): *The Merry Wives of Windsor*

Carl Nielsen (1865–1931): *Maskarade*

Jacques Offenbach (1819–80): *La belle Hélène, Les brigands, The Tales of Hoffmann, La Grande-Duchesse de Gérolstein, Orpheus in the Underworld, La Périchole, La vie parisienne*

Hans Pfitzner (1869–1949): *Palestrina*

Amilcare Ponchielli (1834–86): *La Gioconda*

Francis Poulenc (1899–1963): *Dialogues of the Carmelites, Les mamelles de Tirésias*

Sergei Prokofiev (1891–1953): *The Fiery Angel, The Gambler, The Love for Three Oranges, War and Peace*

Giacomo Puccini (1858–1923): *La bohème, La fanciulla del West, Madama Butterfly, Manon Lescaut, Tosca, Turandot*

Henry Purcell (1659–95): *Dido and Aeneas, The Fairy-Queen, The Indian Queen, King Arthur*

Sergei Rachmaninoff (1873–1943): *Aleko*

Jean-Philippe Rameau (1683–1764): *Les Indes galantes, Platée, Les Boréades*

Maurice Ravel (1875–1937): *L'enfant et les sortilèges, L'heure espagnole*

Nikolai Rimsky-Korsakov (1844–1908): *The Golden Cockerel, Sadko*

Gioacchino Rossini (1792–1868*): Il barbiere di Siviglia, La Cenerentola, Le comte Ory, La donna del lago, Elisabetta, regina d'Inghilterra, La gazza ladra, Guillaume Tell, L'italiana in Algeri, Otello, Semiramide, Il Signor Bruschino, Tancredi, Il turco in Italia, Il viaggio a Reims*

Camille Saint-Saëns (1835–1921): *Samson et Dalila*

Arnold Schoenberg (1874–1951): *Erwartung, Moses und Aron*

Dmitri Shostakovich (1906–1975): *Lady Macbeth of Mtsensk, The Nose*

Bedrich Smetana (1824–1884): *The Bartered Bride*

Ethel Smyth (1858–1944): *The Wreckers*

Karlheinz Stockhausen (1928–): *Licht*

Johann Strauss II (1825–1899): *Die Fledermaus, Der Zigeunerbaron*

Richard Strauss (1864–1949): *Arabella, Ariadne auf Naxos, Capriccio, Elektra, Die Frau ohne Schatten, Intermezzo, Der Rosenkavalier, Salome*

Igor Stravinsky (1882–1971): *The Rake's Progress*

Pyotr Ilyich Tchaikovsky (1840–93): *Iolanta, Mazeppa, The Queen of Spades, Eugene Onegin*

Ambroise Thomas (1811–96): *Hamlet, Mignon*

Virgil Thomson (1896–1989): *Four Saints in Three Acts*

Michael Tippett (1905–98): *The Ice Break, King Priam, The Knot Garden, The Midsummer Marriage*

Mark-Anthony Turnage (1960–): *Greek, The Silver Tassie*

Ralph Vaughan Williams (1872–1958): *The Pilgrim's Progress, Riders to the Sea*

Giuseppe Verdi (1813–1901): *Aida, Un ballo in maschera, Il corsaro, Don Carlos, I due Foscari, Ernani, Falstaff, La forza del destino, Un giorno di regno, Luisa Miller, Macbeth, Nabucco, Otello, Rigoletto, Simon Boccanegra, Stiffelio, La traviata, Il trovatore, Les vêpres siciliennes*

Antonio Vivaldi (1678–1741): *Bajazet, Motezuma, Orlando furioso, Ottone in villa, Tito Manlio*

Richard Wagner (1813–83): *The Flying Dutchman, Götterdämmerung, Lohengrin, Die Meistersinger von*

Nürnberg, Parsifal, Das Rheingold, Rienzi, Der Ring des Nibelungen, Siegfried, Tannhäuser, Tristan und Isolde, Die Walküre

William Walton (1902–83): *Troilus and Cressida*

Carl Maria von Weber (1786–1826): *Abu Hassan, Der Freischütz, Oberon*

Kurt Weill (1900–50): *Rise and Fall of the City of Mahagonny, The Seven Deadly Sins, Street Scene, The Threepenny Opera*

Jaromír Weinberger (1896–1967): *Svanda the Bagpiper*

Judith Weir (1954–): *Blond Eckbert, A Night at the Chinese Opera*

Ermanno Wolf-Ferrari (1876–1948): *Il segreto di Susanna*

Bernd Alois Zimmermann (1918–70): *Die Soldaten*

Lost in translation

A synopsis of Bizet's *Carmen*, provided some years ago by the Paris Opera for the benefit of its English-speaking audience members:

Carmen is a cigar-makeress from a tabago factory who loves with Don José of the mounting guard. Carmen takes a lower from her corsets and lances it to Don José (Duet: 'Talk me of my mother'). There is a noise inside the tabago factory and the revolting cigar-makeresses bursts into the stage. Carmen is arrested and Don José is ordered to mounting guard her but Carmen subduces him and he lets her escape.

ACT 2. The Tavern. Carmen, Frasquita, Mercedes, Zuiniga, Morales. Carmen's aria ('the sistrums are tinkling'). Enter Escamillio, a balls-fighter. Enter two smuglers (Duet: 'We have in mind a business') but Carmen refuses to penetrate because Don Jose has liberated her from prison. He just now arrives (Aria: 'Slop, here who comes!') but hear are the bugles singing his retreat. Don José will leave and draws his sword. Called by Carmen shrieks the two smuglers interfere with her but Don José is bound to dessert, he will follow into them (final chorus: 'Opening sky wandering life')…

AXT 4, a place in Seville. Procession of balls-fighters, the roaring of the balls heard in the arena. Escamillio enters (Aria and chorus: 'Toreador, toreador, All hail the balls of a Toreador'). Enter Don José (Aria: 'I do not threaten, I besooch you') but Carmen repels himwants to join with

Escamillio now chaired by the crowd. Don José stabbs her (Aria: 'Oh rupture, rupture, you may arrest me. I did kill der') he sings "Oh my beautiful Carmen, my subductive Carmen…."

♫ Lost the Plot ♫

The 40 most amazing opera plots

13. *Die Frieschütz* (1821) by Carl Maria von Weber.
A young ranger Max loves Agatha and is likely to become the head ranger. But he needs to prove his shooting skills. But Max has been having a bad month on the shooting range. Caspar, who also loves Agatha, persuades Max to cast some magic bullets to be used in the contest. Caspar's soul is about to be forfeited to the devil but he hopes that by the sacrifice of Max, he'll buy three more years of grace. Scared of losing Agatha, Max goes with Caspar to the wolf's lair to cast the magic bullets. In the forest, Agatha meets a hermit who predicts danger for her but says she'll be protected by her bridal wreath. As the magic bullets are cast, a ghost of Max's mother urges him to abandon the project. At the contest, after successfully discharging six of his bullets, Max's final task is to shoot a dove. As he takes aim, Samiel, a demonic huntsman, guides the bullet, and causes Max to fire at Agatha, who falls down wounded. But her bridal wreath turns the bullet aside and she comes round. Caspar's scheme has failed and he expires with a curse upon his lips. Max confesses all and is given a year's probation after which he can marry Agatha and shoot as much as he likes.

Ten things to know about the Sydney Opera House

1. The original estimated cost for the Sydney Opera House was $7 million. The final cost was $102 million.
2. The building contains 6233 square metres of glass.
3. Eight 747 planes could sit wing to wing on the site.
4. The Grand Organ took ten years to build. It has 10,154 pipes.
5. The Opera House uses up 15,500 light bulbs every year.
6. In 1960 when the Opera House was still being built, Paul Robeson climbed the scaffolding and sang 'Ol' Man River' to the construction workers.
7. Arnold Schwarzenegger won his last Mr Olympia title in the Opera House in 1980.
8. A production of *Boris Godunov* in the 1980s featured live chickens. After one of them wandered off the stage and fell on top of a cellist in the orchestra, a net was installed over the pit.
9. A tapestry in the Opera House's Utzon Room contains 4500 kilometres of wool.
10. An opera *The Eighth Wonder* by Alan John and Dennis Watkins, tells the story of the construction of the Sydney Opera House. It was premièred in the building in 1995.

(Gleaned from www.new7wonders.com)

Hotter's hay fever

The German bass-baritone Hans Hotter (1909–2003) was bedevilled with hay fever during the summer months, greatly affecting his performances in the Bayreuth Festival where he was much in demand as an outstanding Wagnerian performer.

In 1939 in Vienna, Hotter reprised a role he had created the previous year in Richard Strauss's *Friedenstag*. Hotter's hay fever was so debilitating that on the advice of the conductor Clemens Krauss, the singer mimed his part in the dress rehearsal to save his voice for the performance. Legend has it that Strauss told Hotter after the rehearsal that it sounded wonderful. When Hotter protested that he hadn't sung a note, Strauss replied that he had heard in his head how it would sound the following day.

Three years later in 1942, the opening of Richard Strauss's *Capriccio* was postponed to allow Hotter to get over his seasonal blight.

Ten operas based on works by Alexandre Dumas

Some 40 operas have been based on the novels of Alexandre Dumas (1802–70).

1. *Ascanio* (1890) by Camille Saint-Saëns, based on *Benvenuto Cellini*
2. *Gemma di Vergy* (1834) by Donizetti, based on *Charles VII chez ses Grands Vassaux*
3. *Carmelita* (1863) by Pacini, based on *Don Juan de Maraña*
4. *Il Fiore d'Arlem* (1876) by Flotow, based on *Le Tulipe Noir*
5. *Die Drie Musketiere* (1929) by Benatzky, based on *Les Trois Mousquetaires*
6. *Raymond* (1851) by Thomas, based on *The Man in the Iron Mask*
7. *La Mandragore* (1876) by Litolff, based on *Joseph Balsame*
8. *Caterina di Guisa* (1833) by Coccia, based on *Henri III et sa Cour*
9. *Die Heirat wider Willen* (1905) by Humperdinck, based on *Les Demoiselles de St Cyr*
10. *Le Chevalier d'Harmental* (1896) by Messager, based on *Le Chevalier d'Harmental*

Lost the Plot

The 40 most amazing opera plots

14. *Gianni Schicchi* (1918) by Giacomo Puccini.
It is the year 1299. The wealthy Buoso Donati has died and his
relatives have been hovering like vultures around his deathbed. As
soon as he's croaked, they tear the room apart looking for a will.
They're horrified, when they find it, to read that he's left everything
to a bunch of monks. Young Rinuccio is in love with Lauretta, the
daughter of Gianni Schicchi, a shrewd and resourceful peasant.
Rinuccio sends for his future father-in-law and urges the relatives to
consult him about getting out of this situation. Lauretta begs her
beloved daddy to find a solution to the troubles of the family so that
she can marry Rinuccio. Gianni contrives a plot. He removes the
body of Buosi and takes his place in the bed. He then fools the old
man's doctor, saying he is feeling better. Then he listens to what
each relative wants and dictates a new will to a notary. But in this
will he entrusts everything to himself! The relatives are furious
when the notary leaves, but there's nothing they can do. They've
consented to falsifying a will and stand to lose their hands and be
banished out of Florence. The family steal whatever they can and
our hero chases them away. He asks the audience whether Buoso's
money could serve a better purpose and suggests that, although he
will probably go to hell, perhaps the amusement he has afforded
will result in a verdict of extenuating circumstances.

Unsung heroes

Operas that have non-sung moments that are more popular than the work they come from:

The Thieving Magpie (1817) by Gioacchino Rossini. One of Rossini's finest operas is not performed as often as it should be, but its overture is an all-time favourite.

William Tell (1829) by Gioacchino Rossini. The most famous of opera overtures has long been better known than its opera, largely thanks to *The Lone Ranger*.

Die Walküre (1856) by Richard Wagner. The rollicking "Ride of the Valkyries" has stirred audiences worldwide, and was ensured a wider audience through the film *Apocalypse, Now* and in the chase between Elmer Fudd and Bugs Bunny in *What's Opera, Doc?*

Prince Igor (1869) by Alexander Borodin. Borodin died before completing his masterpiece, its colourful orchestrations were completed by Glazunov and Rimsky-Korsakov. The "Polovtsian Dances" in Act II are the opera's most enduring moment.

Cavalleria Rusticana (1890) by Pietro Mascagni. The intermezzo from *Cav* has become a favourite with film-makers, featuring in *Raging Bull* and *The Godfather III* among others.

Thaïs (1894) by Jules Massenet. The "Méditation" from Massenet's opera is played between scenes in Act II. It is one of the best-loved concert pieces for violinists.

Koanga (1904) by Frederick Delius. The dance piece "La

Calinda" from Delius's slavery story is well-loved on record and in the concert hall while the opera *Koanga* is rarely performed.

A Village Romeo and Juliet (1907) by Frederick Delius. "The Walk to the Paradise Garden" links scenes five and six from Delius's Swiss-set opera.

Peter Grimes (1945) by Benjamin Britten. The "Four Sea Interludes" are often performed and well-loved orchestral evocations of the elements.

The Lion King

Operas featuring King Richard I – Richard the Lionheart – of England:

Isacio Tiranno (1710) by Antonio Lotti

Ivanhoe (1891) by Arthur Sullivan

Riccardo Primo (1710) by George Frideric Handel

Richard en Palestine (1844) by Adolphe Adam

Richard Coeur-de-lion (1776) by André-Ernest-Modeste Grétry

Der Templer und die Jüdin (1829) by Heinrich August Marschner

Opera – with whipped cream

One of opera's most colourful and brilliant impresarios, Domenico Barbaia (1775–1841), started life as a waiter in a coffee shop. There he created the *barbaiata*, a cup of coffee or hot chocolate with a frothing, creamy head on it. Taste for his concoction spread and Barbaia opened a chain of cafés serving his trademark beverage.

From coffee, Barbaia moved on to arms dealing and made a fortune buying and selling munitions during the Napoleonic wars. He took over the Teatro San Carlo in Naples in 1809, running it for 13 years. In 1821 he acquired two theatres in Vienna and then five years later ran La Scala, Milan where he commissioned operas from Rossini, Donizetti, Bellini and Weber.

Barbaia also took the legendary mezzo Isabella Colbran as a lover, before she left him for Rossini. Barbaia himself appears as a character in Auber's opera *La Sirène* and was the inspiration for a novel, *Der Impresario* by Emil Luka.

Lost the Plot

The 40 most amazing opera plots

15. *La Gioconda* (1876) by Amilcare Ponchielli.
In Venice, the wicked Barnaba lusts after a street singer who he sees with her blind mother. Barnaba accuses the old woman of witchcraft and an enraged mob threatens her. The powerful Alvise quiets the rabble and his wife Laura begs mercy for the old woman. A banished nobleman Enzo arrives. Our street singer fancies him. But he formerly loved Laura. Barnaba decides he'll win the girl by proving Enzo faithless. He dictates a letter telling Alvise that his wife is going to elope with Enzo. The girl overhears and is distraught. As Enzo and Laura plan to elope, our heroine bursts in. She's about to stab Laura when she realises she's the one who saved her old mum. Unable to harm Laura, the girl tells them to flee. Alvise decides to murder his unfaithful wife. But our heroine replaces the poison with a sleeping draft. Enzo arrives and laments the death of Laura. Alvise orders Enzo's arrest. Our heroine says Barnaba can have his way with her, if he will spare Enzo. Her friends bring the sleeping Laura to her home. Enzo bursts in to kill her for stealing Laura's body, but Laura awakes, and the lovers are reunited. The girl now has to keep her word and face Barnaba. But before he can move she stabs herself. Barnaba screams that he has killed her mother, but the girl no longer hears.

Taking Seville liberties

Operas set in or around Seville include:

Le Nozze di Figaro (1786) by Mozart
Don Giovanni (1787) by Mozart
Fidelio (1805) by Beethoven
La Forza del Destino (1862) by Verdi
Carmen (1875) by Bizet
El gato montés (1916) by Penella
Betrothal in a Monastery (1946) by Prokofiev

Life sentence, or titles of opera stars' autobiographies:

Emma Albani – *Forty Years of Song*
Marian Anderson – *My Lord What a Morning*
Isobel Baillie – *Never Sing Louder Than Lovely*
Janet Baker – *Full Circle*
Thomas Beecham – *A Mingled Chime*
Teresa Berganza – *Flor de Soledad y Silencio*
Jose Carreras – *Singing from the Soul*
Fyodor Chaliapin – *Pages from My Life, Man and Mask*
Regine Crespin – *On Stage, Off Stage*

Placido Domingo – *My First Forty Years*
Geraint Evans – *A Knight at the Opera*
Geraldine Farrar – *Such Sweet Compulsion*
Eileen Farrell – *Can't Help Singing*
Lesley Garrett – *Notes from a Small Soprano*
Joan Hammond – *A Voice, A Life*
Marilyn Horne – *The Song Continues*
Rita Hunter – *Wait Till the Sun Shines, Nellie*
Dorothy Kirsten – *A Time to Sing*
Michael Langdon – *Notes from a Low Singer*
Lilli Lehmann – *Mein Weg*
Frida Leider – *Das war mein Teil*
Christa Ludwig – *In My Own Voice*
Sir Henry Lytton – *The Secrets of a Savoyard*
James McCracken and Sandra Warfield – *A Star in the Family*
Sherrill Milnes – *American Aria: From Farm Boy to Opera Star*
Toti dal Monte – *Una voce nel Mondo*
Grace Moore – *You're Only Human Once*
Tito Schipa – *Si Confessa*
Beverly Sills – *Bubbles: An Encore*
Leo Slezak – *Song of Motley: Being the Reminiscences of a Hungry Tenor*
Elizabeth Söderström – *In My Own Key*
Robert Tear – *Tear Here*
Michael Tippett – *Those Twentieth Century Blues*
Astrid Varnay – *55 Years in Five Acts*
Shirley Verrett – *I Never Walked Alone*
Bruno Walter – *Theme and Variations*

Quotes from Leontyne Price

Born into a segregated black neighbourhood in Mississippi, Leontyne Price overcame intense racial prejudice in the opera world to become one of the outstanding performers of the twentieth century.

"Accomplishments have no colour."

"I am here and you will know that I am the best and will hear me. The color of my skin or the kink of my hair or the spread of my mouth has nothing to do with what you are listening to."

"Art is the only thing you cannot punch a button for. You must do it the old-fashioned way. Stay up and really burn the midnight oil. There are no compromises."

"Onstage, I feel the most beautiful, complete, fulfilled. I think that's why, in the case of noncompromising career women, parts of our personal lives don't work out. One person can't give you the feeling that thousands of people give you."

"The way I was taught, being black was a plus, always. Being a human being, being in America, and being black, all three were the greatest things that could happen to you. The combination was unbeatable."

Le Grande Macabre

Characters in György Ligeti's opera, *La Grande Macabre*:

Piet the Pot
Amando (aka Spermando)
Amanda (aka Clitoria)
Nekrotzar
Astradamors
Mescalina
Venus
Gepopo, Chief of Secret Police
Prince Go-Go
Ruffiack
Schobiack
Schabernack

Lost the Plot

The 40 most amazing opera plots

16. *Un giorno di regno* (1840) by Giuseppe Verdi.
Belfiore – a cavalier – is in France posing as the King of Poland, allowing the real King to travel home and win back his throne. Belfiore arrives at the palace of Baron Kelbar of Brest where he's invited to take part in two weddings. One between Kelbar's daughter Giulietta and La Rocca, and the other between the Baron's niece, the Marchioness of Poggio, and Count Ivrea. But Belfiore's in love with the Marchioness and fears she'll reveal his true identity. La Rocca's nephew Edoardo is in love with Giulietta. Belfiore uses his disguise to help Edoardo by persuading La Rocca not to marry Giulietta. When La Rocca turns his nose up at the nuptials, Kelbar challenges him to a duel. The Marchioness proposes he seek real revenge by marrying Giulietta off to Edoardo. Belfiore, posing as the King, enters and declares it's his right to decide everything. He then orders La Rocca to give Edoardo a castle and allowance in order to end his poverty. The Marchioness and Belfiore confront each other. She tries to make him discard his disguise by faking affection towards the Count. Belfiore pretends to have forgotten her. She's about to promise herself to the Count when Belfiore says he must leave for Poland with the Count at once. Edoardo and Giulietta are in despair because of Edoardo's earlier pledge to follow Belfiore to Poland. A letter arrives from the real King saying he's got home safely and that Belfiore is now appointed Marshal. Still pretending to be the King, Belfiore orders the marriage of Giulietta and Edoardo. He then whips off his disguise, declares himself faithful to the Marchioness and everyone rejoices.

Painting the scenery – famous artists designing for the opera

Marc Chagall (1887–1985). The Russian painter designed numerous opera productions, including *The Magic Flute* at the Metropolitan Opera in New York in 1967. Chagall also provided the ceiling murals at the Paris Opéra, and the foyer paintings for the Met in New York.

Giorgio di Chirico (1888–1978). The Surrealist painter, provided sets for Bellini's *I Puritani* at Florence's May Festival in 1933.

Salvador Dali (1904–89). The Catalan Surrealist, provided peacock feather-inspired sets for a 1950 Covent Garden production of *Salomé*. The press reaction was so hostile that Peter Brook, then head of production, quit his post and stopped producing opera for 30 years.

David Hockney (1937–). The British painter has designed productions of *The Rake's Progress* and *The Magic Flute* for Glyndebourne. For Covent Garden, Hockney designed *Die Frau ohne Schatten, L'Enfant et les Sortilèges* and *The Nightingale*. He also provided designs for *Tristan und Isolde* in Los Angeles.

Oskar Kokoschka (1886–1980). The Austrian expressionist painter provided designs for a number of productions including *The Magic Flute* in Geneva in 1965. He also designed *The Masked Ball* for Florence in 1963.

Henry Moore (1898–1986). He designed a production of *Don Giovanni* at Spoleto in 1976, placing his typical reclining nudes and abstract sculptures around the stage.

John Piper (1903–92). The British painter, designed the first stage productions of Britten's *The Rape of Lucretia, Albert Herring, Billy Budd, Gloriana, The Turn of the Screw, A Midsummer Night's Dream, Owen Wingrave* and *Death in Venice.*

Victor Vasarély (1906–97). The Hungarian-born "op-artist" turned *Tannhauser* into a world of distorted squares that changed colour to suit the seasons, at the Paris Opera in 1984.

Puccini on Paris

On Tuesday 10 May 1898, Giacomo Puccini wrote from Paris where he was getting ready for the première of *La bohème*, to his friend Caselli, a druggist from Luca:

"I am sick of Paris! I am panting for the fragrant woods, for the free movement of my belly in wide trousers and no waistcoat; I pant after the wind that blows free and fragrant from the sea; I savour with wide nostrils its iodic salty breath and stretch my lungs to breathe it!

"I hate pavements! I hate palaces! I hate capitals! I hate columns!

"I love the beautiful columns of the poplar and the fir; I love the vault of shady glades; and I love, like a modern druid, to make my temple my house, my studio therein! I love the green expanse of cool shelter in forest old or young; I love the blackbird, the blackcap, the woodpecker! I hate the horse, the cat, the house sparrow, and the toy dog! I hate the steamer, the top-hat, and the dress-coat!"

Swan Late

Performing in Wagner's *Lohengrin*, tenor Leo Slezak (1873–1946) watched aghast as the swan-boat in which he was meant to be sailing, moved off empty, at the instigation of an over-enthusiastic stage-hand. Slezak's legendary response was to sing, in German, "What time is the next swan?"

Lost the Plot

The 40 most amazing opera plots

17. *The Immortal Hour* (1914) by Rutland Boughton.
Etain, a fairy princess has fallen under the spell of the evil Dalua and doesn't remember anything except her own name. Dalua tells her that the High King of Ireland is drawing near who will find in Etain his heart's desire. The King enters led by dreams and visions to search for his beloved. A spirit voice urges him to return but he is led further into the forest by the promptings of Dalua. A storm erupts and Etain takes shelter in a peasant's hut. The king also arrives at the hut. As soon as he sees Etain he knows his quest is ended. She returns his love. But in a dream, she hears the echoing fairy voices of her own country. A year later, the King calls a feast to celebrate his happiness but Etain is having strange feelings inside – not attributed to last night's curry – and begs to be excused from the celebrations. A stranger arrives saying he is a prince and asks if he may touch the white hand of the Queen with his own lips. The King summons Etain who returns dressed in strange garments. At the touch of the stranger's lips on her hand she recognises him as her true lord, the Prince of Light and Love. Called by irresistible fairy voices, she returns with him to the land of the ever-young. Stricken, the king collapses as the shadow of Dalua covers him completely.

Composer, know thyself

"It is a pity I wrote *Cavalleria* first, I was crowned
before I was king."
Pietro Mascagni (1863–1945)

"Of all composers, past and present, I am the least
learned. I mean what I say in all seriousness, and by
learning I do not mean *knowledge* of music."
Giuseppe Verdi (1813–1901)

"I may not be a first-rate composer, but I *am* a
first-class second-rate composer!"
Richard Strauss (1864–1949)

"My life is to me a deeply interesting romance."
Hector Berlioz (1803–69)

"My heyday is over, and another must take my
place. The world wants something new. Others
have ceded their places to us and we must cede ours
to still others … I am more than happy to give
mine to people of talent like Verdi."
Gaetano Donizetti (1797–1848)

"Give me a laundry list and I will set it to music."
Gioacchino Rossini (1792–1868)

"A man of ordinary talent will always be ordinary,
whether he travels or not; but a man of superior
talent (which I cannot deny myself to be without
being impious) will go to pieces if he remains for
ever in the same place."
Wolfgang Amadeus Mozart (1756–91)

"I write as a sow piddles."
Wolfgang Amadeus Mozart (1756–91)

"I do not play about with empty melodies. I dip
them in life and nature. I find work very difficult
and serious – perhaps for this reason."
Leos Janacek (1854–1928)

"*The Bartered Bride* is only a toy and composing it
was merely child's play!"
Bedrich Smetana (1824–84)

"I remember the first time I tried (composing) the
result looked rather like the Forth Bridge."
Benjamin Britten (1913–76),
quoted in the *Sunday Telegraph*, 1964

"When I compose I always feel I am like
Beethoven; only afterwards do I become aware that
at best I am only Bizet."
Alban Berg (1885–1935)

"I am a different kind of organism, I have hyper-
sensitive nerves, I must have beauty, splendour and
light. The world ought to give me what I need! I
cannot live the wretched life of a town organist like
your Meister Bach! Is it such a shocking demand, if
I believe that I am due the little bit of luxury I
enjoy? I, who have so much enjoyment to give to
the world and to thousands of people!"

Richard Wagner (1813–83)

Lost the Plot

The 40 most amazing opera plots

18. *La Juive* (1835) by Fromental Halévy.
During a holy day festival, Christian townsfolk are shocked to find
that the Jewish goldsmith Eléazar is still working. He's about to be
arrested when a Cardinal calls for forgiveness which he says may
inspire the Jew to turn to Jesus. The Jew's daughter, Rachel is in love
with a painter, Samuel, who is really a married prince called
Léopold. Rachel invites Samuel to join them for a Passover dinner.
After he is almost found out by his wife, Princess Eudoxie, Samuel
tells Rachel that he is a Christian and says the law prescribes death
for any Jewish woman who loves a Christian. She doesn't care and
is about to elope with him when Eléazar catches them. He calls on
God to curse Samuel. Rachel follows Samuel and discovers he is
actually a prince. She publicly announces he's been with a Jewish
girl, a crime for which they both must die. Eudoxie begs Rachel to
spare the man they both love. She does. The cardinal urges her to
save her own life by renouncing her faith, but she refuses. Eléazar
tells the Cardinal that a daughter that he thought had been killed in
a fire is still alive and in the care of a Jew. The Cardinal begs to know
what has become of his daughter. As Rachel is thrown to her death
in a cauldron, Eléazar shouts, 'There's your daughter, Cardinal!'

Peach Melba

The *Peach Melba* – or *Pêche Melba* – was created in honour of the Australian soprano Nellie Melba (1861–1931) by the legendary French chef and restaurateur Auguste Escoffier (1846–1935). Escoffier, who was based at the Savoy Hotel on London's Strand, was inspired after hearing Melba sing at Covent Garden around 1892–93. It was rumoured that Melba did not eat ice cream often because she believed her vocal chords would be affected by it. Escoffier was certain that his vanilla ice cream with peaches, in a sauce made from raspberries, redcurrant jelly, sugar and cornstarch would not be too cold to harm Melba's voice. *Peach Melba* was first served at a dinner that the singer was hosting, served in an ice sculpture of a swan inspired by the performance of *Lohengrin* that Escoffier had seen.

Nellie Melba also gave her name to *Melba toast* – a thinly sliced dry toast, sometimes topped with melted cheese. In 1897, Melba suffered very poor health and it's thought that this snack became a favourite of hers.

Lost the Plot

The 40 most amazing opera plots

19. *Lakmé* (1883) by Léo Delibes.
In India, a priest and his daughter Lakmé – somewhat of a goddess – pray that the Empire-building British will soon leave. As Lakmé bathes, a party of Hooray Henrys burst in. Frédéric – an officer – warns his chums that entering this sacred spot may be seen as sacrilegious. One of the ladies finds the jewels the girl removed when she went to bathe. Gérald, another officer, stays behind to draw the jewels, telling his fiancée that he'll have copies made for their wedding day. Lakmé discovers Gérald and orders him to leave. But, guess what, they fall in love! The priest later realises the garden's been desecrated and swears to kill the culprit. He gets Lakmé to sing in the town hoping that the violator of the sacred garden will recognise her voice and reveal himself. Gérald steps forward and the Priest gets a good look at him. Lakmé persuades Gérald to abandon his regiment and go into hiding with her. Her father bursts from the crowd and stabs Gérald. Lakmé saves him and takes him to a secret jungle bower where she nurses him back to health, accompanied by the cawing of parrots. But Frédéric tracks Gérald down and persuades him to leave. When Lakmé realises Gérald is going, she eats a poisonous flower. The priest bursts in and Lakmé tells him not to kill Gérald; the gods will be satisfied with one victim – herself.

Keep it in the family

Claudio Abbado (1933–), conductor, uncle to **Roberto Abbado** (1954–); brother to **Marcello Abbado** (1926–), composer.

Emil Ábrányi (1882–1970), composer, son of **Emil Ábrányi** (1851–1920), librettist.

Donald Adams (1928–96), bass, husband to **Muriel Harding** (1921–90), soprano.

Norman Bailey (1933–), baritone, husband to **Kristine Ciesinski** (1952–), soprano; brother to **Katherine Bailey** (1950–), mezzo–soprano.

Michael Balfe (1808–70), composer, husband to **Lina Roser** (1808–88), soprano.

Agnes Baltsa (1944–), soprano, erstwhile wife to **Gunter Missenhardt** (1938–), bass.

Rose Bampton (1909–), mezzo, wife to **Wilfrid Pelletier** (1896–1982), conductor.

Samuel Barber (1910–81), composer, nephew to **Louise Homer** (1871–1947), mezzo.

Steuart Bedford (1939–), conductor, erstwhile husband to **Norma Burrowes** (1944–), soprano.

Giuseppina Ronzi de Begnis (1800–53), soprano, wife to **Giuseppe Begnis** (1793–1849), buffo.

Lennox Berkeley (1903–89), composer, father to **Michael Berkeley** (1948–), composer.

Luciano Berio (1925–2006), composer, husband to **Cathy Berberian** (1925–83), soprano.

Walter Berry (1929–), baritone, erstwhile husband to **Christa Ludwig** (1928–), mezzo.

Henry Bishop (1786–1855), composer, husband to **Ann Riviere** (1810–84), soprano.

Georges Bizet (1838–75), composer, son-in-law to **Fromental Halévy** (1799–1862), composer.

Jussi Björling (1911–60), tenor, husband to **Anna-Lisa Berg** (1910–2006), soprano, father to **Rolf Björling** (1937–), tenor.

François-Adrien Boïeldieu (1775–1834), composer, father to **Adrien-Louis-Victor Boïeldieu** (1816–83), composer.

Émmanuel Bondeville (1898–1987), composer, husband to **Viorica Cortez** (1935–), mezzo.

Richard Bonynge (1930–), conductor, husband to **Dame Joan Sutherland** (1927–), soprano.

Faustina Bordoni (1700–81), soprano, wife to **Johann Hasse** (1699–1783), composer.

Christian Bosch (1941–), baritone, son of **Ruthilde Bosch** (1918–), mezzo.

Warwick Braithwaite (1898–1971), conductor, father to **Nicholas Braithwaite** (1939–), conductor.

Marietta Brambilla (1807–75), contralto, sister to **Teresa Brambilla** (1813–95), soprano; aunt to **Teresina Brambilla** (1845–1921), soprano, who was wife to **Amilcare Ponchielli** (1834–86), composer.

Sesto Bruscantini (1919–2003), baritone, erstwhile husband to **Sena Jurinac** (1921–), soprano.

Hans von Bülow (1830–94), conductor, erstwhile husband to **Cosima Liszt** (1837–1930), who left him for **Richard Wagner** (1813–83), composer.

Frantisek Burian (1904–59), composer, nephew of **Karel Burian** (1870–1924), tenor.

Montserrat Caballé (1933–), soprano, wife to **Bernabé Marti** (1934–), tenor.

Giulio Caccini (1545–1618), composer, father to **Francesca Caccini** (1587–1640), composer, and **Settimia Caccini** (1591–1660), soprano.

Cleofonte Campanini (1860–1919), conductor, brother to **Italo Campanini** (1845–96), tenor.

Maria Caniglia (1905–79), soprano, wife to **Pino Donati** (1907–75), artistic director.

Franco Capuana (1894–1969), conductor and composer, brother to **Maria Capuana** (1891–1955), mezzo.

Pietro Antonio Cesti (1623–69), composer, uncle to **Remigio Cesti** (1635–1715), composer.

Luciano Chailly (1920–2002), composer, father to **Riccardo Chailly** (1953–), conductor.

Walter Damrosch (1862–1950), composer and conductor, son of **Leopold Damrosch** (1832–85), conductor.

Paul Daniel (1959–), conductor, husband to **Joan Rodgers** (1956–), soprano.

Hariclea Darclée (1860–1939), soprano, mother to **Ion Hartulary-Darclée** (1886–1969), conductor.

Giacomo Davide (1750–1830), tenor, father to **Giovanni Davide** (1790–1864), tenor, and grandfather to **Giuseppina** (1821–1907), soprano.

Colin Davis (1927–), erstwhile husband of **April Cantelo** (1928–), soprano.

Alfred Deller (1912–79), counter-tenor, father to **Mark Deller** (1938–), counter-tenor.

Murray Dickie (1924–95), tenor, brother to **William Dickie** (1914–85) baritone; father of **John Dickie** (1953–), tenor.

Christoph von Dohnányi (1929–), conductor, grandson
of **Ernö von Dohnányi** (1877–1960), composer;
husband to **Anja Silja** (1935–), soprano; father of
Oliver von Dohnanyi (1955–), conductor.

Willi Domgraf-Fassbaender (1897–1978), baritone,
father of **Birgitte Fassbaender** (1939–), mezzo.

Louise Dugazon (1755–1821), soprano, mother of
Gustave Dugazon (1782–1826), composer.

Leo Fall (1873–1925), composer, brother to **Richard Fall**
(1882–1944), composer.

Charles-Simon Favart (1710–92), librettist, husband to
Marie Favart (1727–72), soprano.

Mafalda Favero (1903–81), soprano, wife to **Alessandro
Ziliani** (1907–77), tenor.

Valentino Fioravanti (1764–1837), composer, father of
Vincenzo Fioravanti (1799–1877), composer.

Joseph Bohuslav Foerster (1859–1951), composer,
husband to **Berta Foestrová-Lautererová** (1869–1936),
soprano.

Alberto Franchetti (1860–1942), composer, father of
Arnold Franchetti (1909–), composer.

Ferdinand Frantz (1906–1959), bass-baritone, husband
to **Helena Braun** (1903–1990), soprano.

Mirella Freni (1935–), soprano, wife to **Nicolai Ghiaurov**
(1929–2004), bass.

Erminia Frezzolini (1818–84), soprano, wife to **Antonio
Poggi** (1806–75), tenor; daughter of of **Giuseppe
Frezzolini** (1789–1861), buffo.

Filippo Galli (1783–1853), tenor, brother to **Vincenzo
Galli** (1798–1858), buffo.

Celestine Galli-Marié (1840–1905), mezzo, daughter of **Félix Mécène Marié de l'Isle** (1811–82), tenor.

Manuel García (1775–1832), tenor, husband to **María Joaquina Sithces** (1780–1854), mezzo; father of **Manuel García** (1805–1906), baritone, **Pauline Viardot-García** (1821–1910), soprano, and **María Malibran** (1808–36), soprano; father-in-law of **Eugénie Mayer** (1815–80), soprano; grandfather of **Gustave García** (1837–1925), baritone.

Angela Gheorghiu (1965–) soprano, wife to **Roberto Alagna** (1963–), tenor.

Beniamino Gigli (1890–1957), father of **Rina Gigli** (1916–), soprano.

Peter Glossop (1928–), baritone, erstwhile husband to **Joyce Blackham** (1934–), mezzo.

Alexander Goehr (1932–), composer, son of **Walter Goehr** (1903–60), composer.

Giulia Grisi (1811–69), soprano, sister to **Giuditta Grisi** (1805–40), mezzo.

Antonio Guarnieri (1880–1952), conductor, father of **Arrigo Guarnieri** (1910–75) and **Ferdinando Guarnieri** (1936–), conductors.

Pietro Guglielmi (1728–1804), composer, father of **Pietro Carlo Guglielmi** (1763–1817), composer.

Håkan Hagegård (1945–), baritone, erstwhile husband to **Barbara Bonney** (1956–) soprano; cousin to **Erland Hagegård** (1944–), tenor.

Michael Haydn (1737–1806), composer, brother to **Franz Joseph Haydn** (1732–1809), composer; husband of **Maria Magdalena Lipp** (1745–1827), soprano.

Victor Herbert (1859–1924) composer, husband to **Therese Foerster** (1861–1927), soprano.

Marilyn Horne (1934–), mezzo, erstwhile wife to **Henry Lewis** (1932–96), conductor; wife of **Nicola Zaccaria** (1923–), bass.

Armas Järnefelt (1869–1958), conductor, brother-in-law to Jean Sibelius (1865–1957), composer; husband to **Maikki Pakarinen** (1871–1929), soprano, and **Liva Edström** (1876–1971) mezzo.

Eugen Jochum (1902–87), conductor, brother to **Georg Jochum** (1909–70), conductor.

Rudolf Kempe (1910–76), conductor, husband to **Elisabeth Lindermeier** (1925–), soprano.

István Kertesz (1929–73), conductor, husband to **Edith Kertesz-Gabry** (1927–), soprano.

Carlos Kleiber (1930–), conductor, son of **Erich Kleiber** (1890–1956), conductor.

Hilde Konetzni (1905–80), soprano, sister to **Anny Konetzni** (1902–68), soprano.

Clemens Kraus (1893–1954), conductor, husband to **Viorica Ursuleac** (1894–1985), soprano.

Ernst Krenek (1900–91), composer, husband to **Gladys Nordenstrom** (1924–), composer.

Jaroslav Krombholc (1918–83), conductor, husband to **Marie Tauberová** (1911–2003), soprano.

Rafael Kubelik (1914–96), conductor, husband to **Elsie Morison** (1924–), soprano.

Benno Kusche (1916–), bass-baritone, husband to **Christine Görner** (1930–), soprano.

Philip Langridge (1939–), tenor, husband to **Ann Murray** (1949–), mezzo.

Giacomo Lauri-Volpi (1892–1979), tenor, husband to
Maria Ros (1895–1970), soprano.

Lilli Lehmann (1848–1929), soprano, sister to Marie
Lehmann (1851–1931); wife to Paul Kalisch
(1855–1946), tenor.

Catarina Ligendza (1937–), soprano, daughter of Einar
Beyron (1901–79), tenor.

Jean-Baptiste Lully (1632–87), composer, father of Louis
Lully (1664–1734), composer.

Sir George MacFarren (1813–87), composer, husband to
Natalia MacFarren (1827–1916), contralto.

Cornell MacNeil (1922–), baritone, father of Walter
MacNeil (1949–), tenor.

Dame Elizabeth Maconchy (1907–94), composer,
mother of Nicola le Fanu (1947–), composer.

Robert Merrill (1917–2004), baritone, erstwhile husband
to Roberta Peters (1930–), soprano.

Mario del Monaco (1915–82), tenor, husband to Rina
Solveni (1918–91), soprano.

Heddle Nash (1894–1961), tenor, father of John Heddle
Nash (1928–94), baritone.

Adelina Patti (1843–1919), soprano, wife to Ernest
Nicolini (1834–98), tenor.

Jan Peerce (1904–84), tenor, brother-in-law to Richard
Tucker (1913–75), tenor.

Fanny Persiani (1812–67), soprano, daughter of Niccolò
Tacchinardi (1772–1850), tenor; wife to Giuseppe
Persiani (1800–69), composer.

Osip Petrov (1806–78), bass, husband to Anna
Yakovlevna Vorobyova (1816–1901), mezzo.

Ezio Pinza (1892–1957), bass, father of **Claudia Pinza** (1927–), soprano.

Lily Pons (1898–1976), soprano, erstwhile wife to **André Kostelanetz** (1901–80), conductor.

Lucia Popp (1939–93), soprano, first married to **György Fischer** (1935–), conductor; secondly married to **Peter Seiffert** (1954–), tenor.

Leontyne Price (1927–), soprano, erstwhile wife to **William Warfield** (1920–2002), bass.

Rosa Raisa (1893–1963), soprano, wife to **Giacome Rimini** (1888–1952), baritone.

Einojuhani Rautavaara (1928–), composer, son of **Eino Rautavaara** (1876–1939), baritone; cousin to **Aulikki Rautavaara** (1906–90), soprano.

Alberto Remedios (1935–), tenor, brother to **Ramon Remedios** (1940–), tenor.

Jean de Reszke (1850–1925), tenor, brother to **Édouard de Reszke** (1853–1917), bass, and **Joséphine de Reszke** (1855–91), soprano.

Elisabeth Rethberg (1894–1976), soprano, wife to **George Cehanovsky** (1892–1986), baritone.

Giorgio Ronconi (1810–90), baritone, brother to **Sebastiano Ronconi** (1814–1900), baritone; son of **Domenico Ronconi** (1772–1839), tenor.

Leonie Rysanek (1926–98), soprano, sister of **Lotte Rysanek** (1928–), soprano.

Marie Sass (1834–1907), soprano, wife to **Armand Castelmary** (1834–97), bass.

Alessandro Scarlatti (1660–1725), composer, father of **Domenico Scarlatti** (1685–1757), composer; great-uncle to **Giuseppe Scarlatti** (1720–1777), composer.

Wilhelmine Schröder-Devrient (1804–60), soprano, daughter of **Friedrich Schröder** (1744–1816), bass.

Ernst von Schuch (1846–1914), conductor, husband to **Klementine Schuch-Proska** (1850–1932), soprano; father of **Liesel Schuch** (1891–1990), soprano.

Elisabeth Schwarzkopf (1915–2006), soprano, wife to **Walter Legge** (1905–79), record producer.

Tullio Serafin (1878–1968), conductor, husband to **Elena Rokowska** (1878–1964), soprano.

José Serebrier (1938–), conductor, husband to **Carole Farley** (1946–), soprano.

Léopold Simoneau (1916–2006), tenor, husband to **Pierette Alarie** (1921–), soprano.

Igor Stravinsky (1882–1971), composer, son of **Fyodor Stravinsky** (1843–1902), bass.

Giuseppina Strepponi (1815–97), soprano, wife of **Giuseppe Verdi** (1813–1901), composer; daughter of **Feliciano Strepponi** (1797–1832), composer.

Pia Tassinari (1903–90), soprano, wife of **Ferrucio Tagliavini** (1913–95), tenor.

Astrid Varnay (1918–2006), soprano, wife of **Hermann Weigert** (1890–1955), conductor.

Ivo Vinco (1928–), bass, husband of **Fiorenza Cossotto** (1935–), mezzo.

Giovanni Zenatello (1876–1949), tenor, husband of **María Gray** (1879–1943), mezzo.

Lost the Plot

The 40 most amazing opera plots

20. *Lohengrin* (1850) by Richard Wagner.
In tenth century Brabant, Count Telramund accuses his ward Elsa of murdering her brother, Gottfried, the heir to the throne. Elsa claims she's dreamed of a knight who'll come to save the war-torn Duchy. Lohengrin appears, pulled in a boat by a swan. Weird. Lohengrin weds Elsa on condition she never ask his name or origin. Weirder. Telramund hates his new rival and has a fight with him. Lohengrin wins and Telramund tries to stop the wedding by saying the unknown knight is an impostor and a sorcerer. That ruse falls flat. Alone on their wedding night, Elsa's anxiety grows until she is compelled to ask her husband who he is – she needs to call him something! Wrong question! Before Lohengrin can reply, Telramund bursts into the bridal chamber without knocking. Lohengrin kills Telramund and sadly tells Elsa he will answer her questions later. He goes off to tell the king he can't lead the army. He says his home is the temple of the Holy Grail to which he must return. He says goodbye and calls for his magic swan which turns into Gottfried, the missing heir to the throne. He thought he was a swan when he was actually an ugly princeling! Lohengrin disappears and Elsa, heartbroken, falls dead to the ground.

The worst use of opera on film

According to the *Encyclopedia of Opera on Screen,* the worst use of opera music in film is found in *Ridin' the Cherokee Trail* (1941) in which Tex Ritter turns arias from *Rigoletto* and *Carmen* into cowboy songs. The opera-loving villain is told by Ritter that 'La donne è mobile' and the 'Toreador Song' really originated on the range. 'La donne è mobile' is in fact a song about Ol' Pete the Bandit, stolen from the cowboys by the "galoot Rigoletto".

Puccini the serial killer

The death toll of Puccini's leading ladies numbers eight in total. "I act as executioner to these poor frail creatures," grinned the composer.

In Puccini's first opera, *Le Villi* (1884), the heroine Anna Wulf doesn't even make it past Act 1. Anna drops dead from grief when she finds out that her fiancé Roberto has fallen for a society lady. At the end of *Edgar* (1889), Fidelia is stabbed by Tigrana, her love rival. Tigrana is executed. The eponymous leading lady of *Manon Lescaut* (1893), deported for being a thief and a prostitute, dies of dehydration in a desert near New Orleans. In *La Boheme* (1896), Mimi succumbs to consumption at the end of Act 4.

Tosca (1900) makes her daring death leap over castle battlements. Cio-Cio San, also known as *Madama Butterfly* (1904), disembowels herself with the same ceremonial sword her father used for his own death. In *Suor Angelica*, the second of three short operas which make up Puccini's trilogy *Il Trittico* (1918), the nun Angelica dies after taking poison herbs when she learns of her illegitimate child's death.

The lucky heroines who make it to the end of a Puccini opera still in one piece are: Minnie, in *La Fanciulla del West* (1910), who rides off with her lover Johnson after saving him from being lynched; Magda, in *La Rondine* (1917), who leaves Ruggero to return to her life as a mistress; Giorgetta, in *Il Tabarro*, the first of *Il Trittico*'s operas, who survives but her lover Luigi is murdered by her husband, Michele; Lauretta, in *Gianni Schicchi*, who lives happily ever after with her lover Rinucio; and Turandot, in the opera of the same name (1926), who even outlived Puccini himself. He died before completing the opera.

Lost the Plot

The 40 most amazing opera plots

21. *Martha* (1847) by Friedrich Flotow.
Lady Harriet is bored with her life at Queen Anne's court. She longs for true love. Hearing the local yokels on their way to the Richmond Fair, she disguises herself and her maid, Nancy so they can go mingle with the peasants. At the fair, girls commit themselves to the service of bidding farmers. Plunkett and Lionel arrive and hire the two ladies as their servants for a year. They're dragged off in a cart to the farmhouse. Once there, the ladies protest that they don't know how to do household chores – it will spoil their hands. Lionel falls for Harriet. And Plunkett for Nancy. But it's all too much for the ladies and they escape at night. Later at a royal hunt, Plunkett spots Nancy and tries to force her back to the farm. Lionel sees Lady Harriet and falls at her feet, professing his love, but, though she loves him, she shuns him for fear of a scandal. Lionel is arrested but gives Plunkett a ring he received from his father and says the Queen must see it. The Queen recognises the ring as that of the unjustly banished Earl of Derby. Lady Harriet is now happy to marry him because he's of good stock. But he rejects her for being two-faced. So the ladies stage a replica of the Richmond Fair and re-enact the earlier events. Plunkett and Lionel can't resist the offers of love.

Good Queen Bess

Ten operas in which Queen Elizabeth I appears:

1. *Il Castello di Kenilworth* (1829) by Gaetano Donizetti
2. *Elisabetta regina d'Inghilterra* (1809) by Stefano Pavesi
3. *Elisabetta in Derbyshire, ossia il castello di Fotheringhay* (1818) by Michele Carafa
4. *Elisabetta, Regina d'Inghilterra* (1815) by Gioacchino Rossini
5. *Elisabeth von England* (1939) by Paul von Klenau
6. *Gloriana* (1953) by Benjamin Britten
7. *Maria Stuarda* (1835) by Gaetano Donizetti
8. *Merrie England* (1902) by Edward German
9. *Roberto Devereux* (1837) by Gaetano Donizetti
10. *Le Songe d'une Nuit d'Été* (1850) by Ambroise Thomas

Unexpected librettists

A list of some major writers and some unexpected interlopers who've contributed the words for operas:

Hans Christian Anderson (1805–1875), the fairy-tale author, provided the libretti for four Danish operas.

W.H. Auden (1907–1973), Anglo-American poet, penned the libretto for Henze's *Elegy for Young Lovers* and *The Bassarids*, *Paul Bunyan* for Benjamin Britten, *The Rake's Progress* for Stravinsky, and *Love's Labour's Lost* for Nicolas Nabokov.

Arnold Bennett (1867–1931), British novelist, wrote the libretto for Eugene Goosens' *Judith*, in which Joan Sutherland made her debut in 1951.

Ingmar Bergman (1918–2007), Swedish film director, provided the words for Daniel Börtz's *The Bacchae*, which Bergman also directed.

Catherine the Great of Russia (1729–96) gave libretti to her court composer Vasily Alexeyevich for three operas, including *The Early Reign of Oleg*.

Colette (1873–1954), French writer, provided the words for Ravel's *L'enfant et les sortileges*, but had little personal contact with the composer.

Charles Dickens (1812–70), English novelist, wrote the words for his friend John Pyke Hullah's *The Village Coquettes*.

Frederick the Great of Prussia (1712–86) presented the Kappellmeister of the Berlin Opera, Carl Heinrich Graun, with the libretti for four operas.

E.M. Forster (1879–1970), English writer, collaborated with Eric Crozier on the libretto for Britten's *Billy Budd*.

Ted Hughes (1930–98), English poet, wrote the words for Gordon Crosse's *The Story of Vasco*.

Oskar Kokoschka (1886–1980), Austrian expressionist painter, provided the libretti for Hindemith's *Mörder, Hoffnung der Frauen* and Krenek's *Orpheus und Eurydike*.

Clemens Krauss (1893–1954), a conductor, helped write the libretto for Richard Strauss's *Capriccio*.

Francis Burdett Money-Coutts (1852–1923), London banker, became patron to Isaac Albeniz on condition that Albeniz used Money-Coutts's own librettos for his operas. Together they wrote *Henry Clifford*, *Merlin*, and *Pepita Jiménez*.

J.B. Priestley (1894–1984), English writer, wrote the words for Arthur Bliss's *The Olympians*.

Franco Zeffirelli (1923–), Italian director, wrote the libretto for Samuel Barber's *Antony and Cleopatra*.

Lost the Plot

The 40 most amazing opera plots

22. *Il Matrimonio Segreto* (1792) by Domenico Cimarosa.
This is the story of a man called Geronimo, a wealthy, deaf, Bolognese merchant. Geronimo has two daughters – Elisetta and Carolina. Their household is run by his sister, Fidalma. Carolina is secretly married to Paolino, who Fidalma fancies. Count Robinson arrives to marry Elisetta but falls for Carolina who tries to repel him by talking of her many faults, but he's not convinced. Geronimo is delighted at the Count's apparent interest in Elisetta and organises a banquet in his honour. At the banquet, the Count convinces Geronimo of his interest in Carolina. Paolino goes to Fidalma to help them out, but she misinterprets his words as a proposal of marriage and he faints into her arms. Carolina enters at that moment and takes some convincing of Paolino's love for her. The count seeks to estrange Elisetta by painting himself as an ogre, a kind of operatic Shrek. She and Fidalma respond by trying to send Carolina to a convent. Paolino and Carolina decide to run away but are caught by Elisetta who summons the household. The assumption is that the man with Carolina is the Count but he makes a surprise entrance from another room. Paolino and Carolina confess their marriage. The Count agrees to marry Elisetta and all ends happily.

Classification of singers

The Fach system is a means of categorising opera singers by the range, weight, and colour of their voices. It is mostly used in German-speaking opera companies. Singers who are classified as being of a certain Fach are usually only offered roles that come within that Fach. Here is a list of Fächer, their English equivalent and their ranges.

Coloratura Fächer

Lyrischer Koloratursopran or Koloratursoubrette. Coloratura soprano or Lyric Coloratura soprano. A light soprano with a  high, acrobatic voice, such as Beverly Sills or Edita Gruberova. Roles include Gilda in *Rigoletto* and *Lucia di Lammermoor.*

Dramatischer Koloratursopran. Dramatic coloratura soprano. A rich, dramatic voice capable of ornamentation, such as Maria  Callas or Joan Sutherland. Roles include the Queen of the Night in *The Magic Flute* and *Violetta* in *La Traviata.*

Soprano Fächer

Deutsche Soubrette or Charaktersopran. Soubrette. A light, pretty voice such as Dawn

Upshaw or Kathleen Battle. Roles include Susanna in *The Marriage of Figaro* and Zerlina in *Don Giovanni*.

Lyrischer Sopran. Lyric soprano. An agile and more sensuous voice such as Angela Gheorghiu, Renée Fleming or Kiri te Kanawa. Roles include Mimi in *La bohème* and Micaela in *Carmen*.

Jugendlich Dramatischer Sopran. Light dramatic soprano. Known as a *spinto* in Italian, this singer must be able to push her lighter voice at times to create a bigger sound, such as Leontyne Price or Gundula Janowitz. Roles include Cio-Cio San in *Madama Butterfly* or Floria Tosca in *Tosca*.

Dramatischer Sopran. Full dramatic soprano. Must be able to cope with demanding roles such as Leonore in *Fidelio* or Lady Macbeth in *Macbeth*. Singers in this fach include Helga Dernesch and Jessye Norman.

Hochdramatischer Sopran. Wagnerian soprano. A substantial voice that can meet the demands of Wagner's roles, such as Brunnhilde or Isolde, or Turandot. Singers in this fach include Birgit Nilsson, Kirsten Flagstad or Eva Turner.

Mezzo-soprano Fächer

Lyrischer Mezzosopran or Spielalt. Lyric mezzo-soprano. A sensitive lyric soprano voice with a lower range suitable for  Carmen, Cherubino in *The Marriage of Figaro* or Octavian in *Der Rosenkavalier*. Singers include Janet Baker, Christa Ludwig or Anne-Sofie von Otter.

Koloratur-Mezzosopran. Coloratura mezzo-soprano. As above but capable of vocal fireworks, as in Rosina in *The*  *Barber of Seville*. Singers include Cecilia Bartoli or Conchita Supervía.

Dramatischer Mezzosopran. Dramatic mezzo-soprano. A large middle-range voice capable of full-bodied projection as in  Amneris in *Aida,* Eboli in *Don Carlo* or Ortrud in *Lohengrin*. Singers include Grace Bumbry.

Dramatischer Alt. Contralto. A deep, penetrating female voice. Roles include Erda in Wagner's *Ring*.

Tiefer Alt. Contralto. A very rare voice type with a richer sound. Roles include Ulrica in *Un ballo in maschera*. Singers  include Marian Anderson, Clara Butt or Kathleen Ferrier.

Tenor Fächer

Spieltenor or Tenor Buffo. Lyric comic tenor. A young Spieltenor could become a Lyrischertenor, depending on his voice and looks. Roles include Pedrillo in *Die Entführing aus dem Serail*.

Charaktertenor. Character tenor. Must have good acting abilities, as in Mime in Wagner's *Siegfried*. Singers include Gerhard Stolze.

Lyrischer Tenor. Lyric tenor. A clear pure voice to be able to sing roles like Tamino in *The Magic Flute*. Singers in this fach include Ian Bostridge, Alfredo Kraus and Richard Tauber.

Jugendlicher Heldentenor or Falscher Heldentenor. Light dramatic tenor, possessing a dramatic voice and high upper range which is able to cut through and above an orchestra. Roles include Don José in *Carmen, Parsifal* or *Lohengrin*. Singers include Plácido Domingo.

Echter Heldentenor. German dramatic tenor, a full dramatic voice with strong middle range. Roles include *Otello* and Tristan in *Tristan und Isolde*. Singers include Jon Vickers, Ben Heppner or Mario del Monaco.

III

Baritone Fächer

Lyrischer Bariton or
Spielbariton. Lyric baritone. A
sweeter baritone voice for roles
such as Marcello in *La bohème*. Singers include Dietrich
Fischer-Dieskau and Hermann Prey.

Kavalierbariton. A flexible voice
that can cope with both lyric and
dramatic phrases. Roles include
Don Giovanni and Iago in *Otello*. Singers in this fach
include Thomas Hampson, Dmitri Hvorostovsky and
Sherrill Milnes.

Charakterbariton. Verdi
Baritone. Strong flexible voice
with powerful appearance on
stage, for Verdi roles and *Wozzeck*. Singers include
Matthias Goerne and Titta Ruffo.

Hoherbass. High bass or bass-
baritone, midway and varying in
pitch between baritone and bass.
Roles include Caspar in *Die Freischutz* or Mephistopheles
in *Faust*. Singers include Ezio Pinza and Cesare Siepi.

Heldenbariton. Heroic baritone.
Germans especially prize the
Heldenbariton who has great
power and brilliance in roles such as Telramund in
Lohengrin, or Count di Luna in *Il trovatore*. Singers
include Leonard Warren.

Bass Fächer

Bassbariton. Bass-baritone. A varied range depending on the role, includes Figaro in *The Marriage of Figaro* or Wotan in Wagner's *Ring*. Singers include Samuel Ramey, Bryn Terfel and Hans Hotter.

Spielbass or Bassbuffo. A lyric comic bass, that requires character acting skills, for roles such as *Don Pasquale*. Singers include Luigi Lablache and Andrew Shore.

Schwerer Spielbass. Dramatic comic bass that can take roles such as Baculus in *Der Wildschütz*.

Seriöser Bass. Dramatic (serious) bass or Basso Profundo. A deep and powerful voice that can cope with roles such as *Boris Godunov* or Sarastro in *The Magic Flute*. Singers include Feodor Chaliapin, Boris Christoff, Kurt Moll or Martti Talvela.

Lost the Plot

The 40 most amazing opera plots

23. *Mignon* (1866) by Ambroise Thomas.

This is the story of a well-to-do young lady who's abducted by travellers. Her father loses his marbles and wanders about disguised as a minstrel searching for her (and his marbles presumably). The gipsy leader treats the girl very cruelly, making her dance in public. Wilhelm, a travelling student, takes pity on her and ransoms her from the gypsies. She falls head over heels for Wilhelm but he doesn't notice because he fancies an actress called Philine. Philine is called to do a gig at a castle. The audience adore her and Wilhelm's passions are aroused even more. Our heroine – who's also there in disguise – is consumed with jealousy. Her father appears in his minstrel costume and they don't recognise each other. She tells the minstrel all her woes and says she wishes the castle would burn down. Sure enough, being a little unhinged, he sets it alight. Wilhelm rescues her from the burning debris. Back at her father's mansion in a delirious state, she mumbles about loving Wilhelm. Her father finally recognises her and regains his sanity. Wilhelm decides that its hard work being in love with an actress and is ready to return our heroine's love.

Singers' nicknames

Maria Callas (Greek soprano) . . . . La Divina
Adriana Gabriele (Italian soprano) . . . . La Ferrarese
Jenny Lind . . . . The Swedish Nightingale
(Swedish soprano)
Mario del Monaco . . . . The Brass Bull of Milan
(Italian tenor)
Patrice Munsel (American soprano) . . . . Princess Pat
Jessye Norman (American soprano) . . . . . . Just Enormous
Ernestine Schumann-Heink . . . . . Madam Human Shank
(Czech contralto)
Frederick von Stade . . . . Flicka
(American mezzo)
Joan Sutherland (Australian soprano) . . . . . . La Stupenda
Titta Ruffo (Italian baritone) . . . . Voce del leone
(Voice of the lion)

Miaow!

"I could not compose operas like *Don Giovanni*
and *Figaro*. I hold them both in aversion. I could
not have chosen such subjects; they are too
frivolous for me."
Ludwig van Beethoven (1770–1827)

"I like your opera – I think I will set it to music."
Ludwig van Beethoven, after hearing an
opera by another composer

"Berlioz says nothing in his music but he says
it magnificently."
James Gibbons Huneker (1860–1921),
Old Fogy, 1913

"Music for sluts."
Wagner on Gounod's *Faust*

"It's beautiful and boring. Too many pieces finish
too long after the end."
Stravinsky on Handel's *Theodora*

"I consign it from the bottom of my heart to the devil;
it is the most insipid and base parody on music."
Tchaikovsky on Mussorgsky's
Boris Godunov

"(Mussorgsky's) nature is not of the finest quality;
he likes what is coarse, unpolished, and ugly."
Peter Ilyich Tchaikovsky
(1840–1893)

"We know butter is made from cream, but do we
have to watch it being churned?"
Charles Ives on Tchaikovsky's
Eugene Onegin

"A tub of pork and beer."
Berlioz on Handel,
quoted in Elliott, *Berlioz*, 1967

"Lamentably provincial."
Stravinsky on Shostakovich's
Lady Macbeth of Mtsensk

Shostakovich: "What do you think of Puccini?"
Britten: "I think his operas are dreadful."
Shostakovich: "No, Ben, you are wrong. He wrote
marvellous operas, but dreadful music."
Quoted in Harewood,
The Tongs and the Bones, 1981

"Abominably commonplace."
Vincent d'Indy on *Pagliacci*
by Leoncavallo

"A highly unsavoury stirring-up together of Israel,
Africa and the Gaelic isles ...
gefilte fish orchestration."

Virgil Thompson on
Gershwin's *Porgy and Bess*

"Listening to the fifth symphony of Ralph Vaughan
Williams is like staring at a cow for 45 minutes."

Aaron Copland

"The audience ... expected the ocean. Something
big, something colossal, but they were served
instead with some agitated water in a saucer."

Louis Schneider on Debussy's *La Mer*

"What a good thing this isn't music."

Rossini on Berlioz's *Symphonie Fantastique*

"He's not a composer – he's a kleptomaniac."

Stravinsky on Britten

Lost the Plot

The 40 most amazing opera plots

24. *Norma* **(1831) by Vincenzo Bellini.**
In Gaul, at the time of Asterix and Obelix, the Druid's High Priest prays for help to defeat the Romans. But his daughter, Norma, the High Priestess has been the secret lover of the Roman leader Pollione. She's broken her chastity vow and had two children with him. Norma hopes to save Pollione's life but he wants to dump her now, because he fancies a temple virgin, Adalgisa. Adalgisa goes to pray but finds herself face to face with Pollione, who seduces her. She goes to see Norma and both women betray the truth about themselves. Norma is so distraught that she contemplates killing her children rather than let them be taken to Rome as slaves. Adalgisa refuses to come between Norma and Pollione, and the two women vow that nothing shall destroy their friendship. But Pollione only wants Adalgisa. Furious, Norma tells the Gauls that the gods will support an attack on the Romans. Pollione is captured trying to break into Norma's sanctuary. She admits to her people that she has dishonoured her sacred vows and deserves to be killed. She begs her father to forgive her and take care of her children. She's led away by the Gauls while Pollione resolves to die beside the woman he has loved and betrayed.

Chaos instead of music

Dmitri Shostakovich was enjoying great success with his opera, *Lady Macbeth of Mtsensk*. In January 1936, three productions of it were playing in Moscow. On 26 January, Mr and Mrs Joseph Stalin attended a performance. Stalin refused to meet Shostakovich and left the theatre before the last act. Two days later, reading the latest edition of *Pravda*, Shostakovich saw this review under the headline "Chaos instead of music":

Certain theatres are presenting to the new culturally mature Soviet public Shostakovich's opera *Lady Macbeth* as an innovation and achievement. Musical criticism, always ready to serve, has praised the opera to the skies, and given it resounding glory. The young composer, instead of hearing serious criticism, which could have helped him in his future work, hears only enthusiastic compliments.

From the first minute, the listener is shocked by deliberate dissonance, by a confused stream of sound. Snatches of melody, the beginnings of a musical phrase, are drowned, emerge again, and disappear in a grinding and squealing roar. To follow this "music" is most difficult; to remember it, impossible.

Thus it goes, practically throughout the entire opera. The singing on the stage is replaced by shrieks. If the composer chances to come upon the path of a clear and simple melody, he throws himself back into a wilderness of musical chaos – in places becoming cacophony. The expression which the listener expects is supplanted by wild rhythm. Passion is here supposed to be expressed by noise. All this is not due to lack of talent, or lack of ability to depict strong and simple emotions in music. Here is music turned deliberately inside out in order that nothing will be reminiscent of classical opera, or have anything in common with symphonic music or with simple and popular musical language accessible to all.

... The composer of Lady Macbeth was forced to borrow from jazz its nervous, convulsive, and spasmodic music in order to lend "passion" to his characters. ... all this is coarse, primitive and vulgar. The music quacks, grunts, and growls, and suffocates itself in order to express the love scenes as naturalistically as possible. And "love" is smeared all over the opera in the most vulgar manner. The merchant's double bed occupies the central position on the stage. On this bed all "problems" are solved. In the same coarse, naturalistic style is shown the death from poisoning and the flogging – both practically on stage.

... Our theatres have expended a great deal of energy on giving Shostakovich's opera a thorough presentation. The actors have shown exceptional talent in dominating the noise, the screaming, and the roar of the orchestra. With their dramatic action, they have tried to reinforce the weakness of the melodic content. Unfortunately, this has served only to bring out the opera's vulgar features more vividly. The talented acting deserves gratitude, the wasted efforts – regret.

Actors playing opera composers

Beethoven. Fritz Kortner in *Beethoven's Lebensroman* (1918) and *The Life of Beethoven* (1927), Henry Baur in *Un grand amour de Beethoven* (1936), Albert Basserman in *New Wine* (1941) (known as *The Melody Master* in the USA), Memo Benassi in *Rossini* (1942), Ewald Balser in *Eroica* (1949), Erich von Stroheim in *Napoleon* (1954), Karl Böhm in *The Magnificent Rebel* (1961–2), Donatas Banionis in *Beethoven – Tage aus einem Leben* (1970), Wolfgang Reichmann in *Beethoven's Nephew* (1985), Gary Oldman in *Immortal Beloved* (1995), Ian Hart in *Eroica* (2003), Ed Harris in *Copying Beethoven* (2006). The film *Beethoven* (1992) is not about Ludwig van Beethoven at all, but a disaster-prone St. Bernard dog.

Bellini. Phillips Holmes in *The Divine Spark* (1935), Sandro Palmieri in *Casta Diva* (1935), Roberto Villa in *La sonnambula* (1942), Roberto Bruni in *Maria Malibran* (1943), Maurice Ronet in *Casa Ricordi* (1954) and *Casta Diva* (1954), Enrico De Melis in *Un palco all'opera* (1955), Kim Rossi Stuart in *La famiglia Ricordi* (1993).

Berlioz. Jean-Louis Barrault in *La Symphonie Fantastique* (1940), Corin Redgrave in *I, Berlioz* (1992).

Boito. Carlo Duse in *Puccini* (1952), Denny Cecchini in *La famiglia Ricordi* (1993).

Donizetti. Lamberto Picasso in *Giuseppe Verdi* (1938), Amadeo Nazzari in *Il cavakuere del sogno* (1946), Marcello Mastroianni in *Casa Ricordi* (1954), Fausto

Tozzi in *Casta Diva* (1954), Eduardo De Santis in *Un palco all'opera* (1955), Alessandro Gassman in *La famiglia Ricordi* (1993).

Gershwin. Robert Alda in *Rhapsody in Blue* (1945).

Gilbert and Sullivan. Nigel Bruce and Claud Allister in *Lillian Russell* (1941), Robert Morley and Maurice Evans in *The Story of Gilbert and Sullivan* (1953), Jim Broadbent and Allan Corduner in *Topsy Turvy* (1999).

Grieg. Toalv Maurstad in *Song of Norway* (1970).

Handel. Wilfred Lawson in *The Great Mr. Handel* (1942), Simon Callow in *Honour, Profit and Pleasure* (1985), Trevor Howard in *God Rot Tunbridge Wells!* (1985).

Lully. Mario Gonzales in *Moliere* (1978), Boris Terral in *Le Roi danse* (2000).

Mercadante. Maurizio D'Ancora in *Casta Diva* (1935).

Mozart. Josef Zetenius in *Mozarts Leben, Lieben und Leiden* (1921), Stephen Haggard in *Whom the Gods Love* (1936), Hannes Steltzer in *Eine Kleine Nachtmusik* (1939), Gino Cervi in *Melodie eterne* (1939), Hans Holt in *Wen die Götter lieben* (1942) and *The Mozart Story* (1948), Oskar Werner in *Reich mir die Hand, mein Leben* (1955), Richard La Bonte in *Mozart in Love* (1975), Christopher Davidson in *Noi tre* (1984), Tom Hulce in *Amadeus* (1984), Max Tidof in *Vergesst Mozart* (1985).

Mussorgsky. Lewis Howard in *Song of My Heart* (1948), Alexander Borisov in *Mussorgsky* (1950).

Puccini. Gabriele Ferzetti in *Puccini* (1953), Gabriele Ferzetti in *Casa Ricordi* (1954), Albert Lionello in *Puccini* (1973), Robert Stephens in *Puccini* (1984), Massimo Ghini in *La famiglia Ricordi* (1993).

Rimsky-Korsakov. Jean-Pierre Aumont in *Song of Scheherezade* (1947), David Leonard in *Song of My Heart* (1948), Grigori Belov in *Rimsky-Korsakov* (1952).

Rossini Achille Majeroni in *Casta Diva* (1935), Edmond Breon in *The Divine Spark* (1935), Nino Bessozi in *Rossini* (1943), Loris Gizzi in *Maria Malibran* (1943), Roland Alexandre in *Casa Ricordi* (1954), Augusto Di Giovanni in *Un palco all'opera* (1955), Philippe Noiret in *Rossini! Rossini!* (1991), Luca Barbareschi in *La famiglia Ricordi* (1993), Joe Dimambro in *Rossini's Ghost* (1996).

Salieri. Wilton Graff in *The Mozart Story* (1948), Albin Skoda in *Reich mir die Hand, mein Leben* (1955), F. Murray Abraham in *Amadeus* (1984), Winfried Glatzeder in *Vergesst Mozart* (1985).

Shostakovich. Ben Kingsley in *Testimony* (1988).

Johann Strauss II. Johann Strauss (the composer's nephew) in *Ein Walzer vom Strauss* (1925), Imre Raday in *Heut spielt der Strauss* (1929), Hans Stuwe in *Der Walzerkönig*, Gustav Frölich in *A Waltz from Strauss* (1931), Michael Bohnen in *Johann Strauss, Hofballmusikdirektor* (1932), Esmond Knight in *Waltzes from Vienna* (1933), Fernand Gravet in *The Great Waltz* (1938), Alfred Jerger in *Unsterbliche Melodien* (1938), Bernhard Wicki in *Ewiger Walzer* (1954), Keith Andes in *The Great Waltz* (1955), Kerwin Matthews in *The Waltz King* (1960), Horst Buchholz in *The Great Waltz* (1972), Stuart Wilson in *The Strauss Family* (1972), Michael Riley in *Strauss: The King of Three-Quarter Time* (1996).

Tchaikovsky. Frank Sundstrom in *Song of my Heart* (1947), Innokenti Smoktunovsky in *Tchaikovsky* (1970),

Richard Chamberlain in *The Music Lovers* (1971), Vladimir Ashkenazy in *Tchaikovsky* (1986).

Verdi. Leopoldo Fregoli in *Maestri di musica* (1898), Paolo Rosmino in *Giuseppe Verdi nella Vita e nella Gloria* (1913), Fosco Giachetti in *Giuseppe Verdi* (1938), Fosco Giachetti in *Casa Ricordi* (1954), Pierre Cressoy in *Verdi, The King of Melody* (1953), Ronald Pickup in *The Life of Verdi* (1982), Mariano Rigillo in *La Famiglia Ricordi* (1993).

Wagner. Giuseppe Becce in *Richard Wagner* (1913), Alan Badel in *Magic Fire* (1956), Lyndon March in *Song Without End* (1960), Trevor Howard in *Ludwig* (1973), Paul Nicholas in *Lisztomania* (1975), Richard Burton in *Wagner* (1983), Otto Sander in *Richard and Cosima* (1987).

Lost the Plot

The 40 most amazing opera plots

25. *Pagliacci* (1892) by Ruggero Leoncavallo.
A band of travelling players arrive in a small Italian town. Canio, the head of the troupe, is married to Nedda. The hunchback Tonio appears and tries to seduce Nedda but she lashes out at him with a whip and he gets somewhat peeved. Nedda's real lover — Silvio – wants her to run away with him. The spurned hunchback lurches off to tell Canio. The jealous husband bursts in on the guilty pair but Silvio escapes and Nedda refuses to name him, even when he threatens her with a knife. Another player, Beppe has to restrain Canio who sobs that he has to go on and play the clown even though his heart is broken. In the performance, Colombina – played by Nedda – is serenaded by her lover – played by Beppe. They plot to poison her husband the clown – played by Canio – who soon arrives. The clown is assured of his wife's innocence. But Canio's real-life jealousy increases. Discarding the script, he demands that Nedda reveal her lover's name. She tries to continue with the play – the audience think it's all terribly realistic. Bravo! they cry. But Canio stabs Nedda *and* Silvio when he rushes from the crowd to help her. Well, the show must go on – except the actors are dead!

It's time to raise the curtain ...

What are the connections between opera and the Muppets? Well…

Renée Fleming appeared on *Sesame Street*, singing 'Caro nome' from Verdi's *Rigoletto*, with the normal words replaced by new lyrics to help children count to five. Miss Piggy and the pigs sang 'I want to sing in opera' in an episode of *The Muppet Show*. Marilyn Horne sang 'C is for cookie' dressed as Cleopatra in an episode of *Sesame Street*. In another episode of *The Muppet Show*, "Marilyn Horn" is a trumpet in a blonde wig. Beverly Sills was a guest on the show, performing in *Pigoletto*. Before the performance began, a pig duo appears in Sills's wardrobe to audition, with the 'Anvil Chorus'. The Great Gonzo also attempted to demolish a car to the 'Anvil Chorus' while two flat-faced muppets struck their heads against anvils to it in an episode of *Muppets Tonight*. Fozzie Bear and a matador have performed 'The Toreador Song'. Miss Piggy and Link Hogthrob sang 'La Ci Darem La Mano' from *Don Giovanni*. A giant magnet pulls them in their metal costumes off the stage. In episode 213 of *The Muppet Show*, Giuseppe Wagner is the fictional composer of *The Barber of Die Fledermaus*. The most regular operatic muppet was Placido Flamingo, an opera-singing flamingo on *Sesame Street*, who was seen singing in the Nestopolitan Opera House's "Live from the Nest" series. Flamingo performed a duet with the real Domingo in the show's 20th anniversary special. Placido Domingo also duetted with Miss Piggy in the 1982 *Night of 100 Stars* special. An enormous opera singer, modeled on Brunnhilde, appeared in *Sesame Street*. She sang 'Everything's Coming up Noses'. A group of chickens cluck Wagner's 'Ride of the Valkyries' in episode 106 of *Muppets Tonight*. Sweetums growled the same tune to John Cleese in a horned-helmet when he guested on *The Muppet Show*. The chickens returned to cluck the overture for *William Tell* as the Great Gonzo performed a water-skiing stunt in *The Muppets take Manhattan*.

The Muppet Zubin Beckmesser is leader of New York City's Metropolitan Opera. In a *Muppet Show* news item it's reported that Beckmesser has been electrocuted when he inserted his baton into an electrical outlet. According to doctors, he would have died instantly had he not been such a poor conductor. Groan.

Ten Operas based on works by Victor Hugo

Some 75 operas have been inspired by the works of French writer Victor Hugo (1802–1885).

1. *Rigoletto* (1851) by Verdi, based on *Le Roi s'Amuse*
2. *Lucrezia Borgia* (1833) by Donizetti, based on *Lucrèce Borgia*
3. *Picarol* (1901) by Granados, based on *Notre-Dame de Paris*
4. *La Giaconda* (1876) by Ponchielli, based on *Angélo, Tyran de Padoue*
5. *Ernani* (1844) by Verdi, based on *Hernani*
6. *Han d'Islande* (1856) by Moussorgsky, based on *Han d'Islande*
7. *The Comedians* (1920) by Enna, based on *L'Homme qui Rit*
8. *Isora di Provenza* (1884) by Mancinelli, based on *La Légende des Siècles*
9. *Maria Tudor* (1843) by Pacini, based on *Marie Tudor*
10. *Las Hijas del Batallón* (1898) by Chapí, based on *Quatre-Vingt-Treize*

Sopranos at war

Francesca Cuzzoni (1700–70), one of the great Italian sopranos of her time, had a bitter rivalry with Faustina Bordoni, both of them egged on by their fans.

The singers' contempt for each other erupted into a public conflagration in 1727 when audience catcalls and whistling led to the two of them exchanging real blows and pulling each other's hair, during a London production of Bononcini's opera, *Astianatte*. The curtain came down and supporters of the rival singers threw chairs at each other.

Cuzzoni was dismissed by the Royal Academy but reinstated when the King said he would withdraw his personal subsidy to the Academy. Both Cuzzoni and Bordoni were booked to return the next season. Their rivalry inspired the characters of Polly Peachum and Lucy Lockit in John Gay's *The Beggar's Opera*.

On another occasion when Cuzzoni refused to sing an aria for Handel, the composer yelled at her, "I well know that you are truly a She-Devil: but I will have you know that I am Beelzebub, chief of the Devils". Handel wanted Cuzzoni to be dangled upside down from a window until she agreed to sing.

Cuzzoni suffered a sad fall from grace, accused of poisoning her husband, imprisoned for debt in Holland, and eventually resorted to selling buttons to scrape together a meagre living. She died in poverty.

Lost the Plot

The 40 most amazing opera plots

26. *Il pirata* (1827) by Vincenzo Bellini.
The pirate Gualtiero has been defeated in a sea battle by Ernesto, a Sicilian Duke. Shipwrecked, Gualtiero hides away so he's not discovered by his enemies. Ernesto's wife, Imogene arrives and is told that Gualtiero may have been lost at sea. She's heartbroken because he's her old flame. Gualtiero comes out of hiding and accuses her of betraying him. She says she had to marry the Duke to save her aged father from death in prison. The Duke returns and can't understand why Imogene seems depressed after his sea victory. Ernesto questions the shipwrecked survivors and realises they come from a place which sheltered Gualtiero and the pirates. Imogene begs him to let them leave the next morning. He agrees but Gualtiero leaps out and onto Ernesto. The guards capture him and he is dragged off by his shackles. Imogene tells Ernesto she still loves Gualtiero. But she's not prepared to dishonour her marriage vows. Ernesto goes off to kill Gualtiero but in the scuffle, gets himself killed. Gualtiero readily gives himself up to face justice. Imogene slowly goes mad. Hearing the trumpet sound Gualtiero being condemned to the gallows, she declares herself ready to die too, of grief.

The tragic case of Puccini's maid

Puccini had a complex relationship with his wife, Elvira with whom he had eloped while she was still married to another man. In 1909, Elvira inexplicably became convinced that Puccini was having an affair with their 21-year-old maid, a simple village girl named Doria Manfredi. Elvira launched a malicious campaign of lies, driving Doria away and harassing her publicly to the point that the girl poisoned herself and died after almost a week of agony. A post mortem was performed and proved that Doria was still a virgin. After a case of persecution and calumny was brought by Doria's family, Elvira – still maintaining her tirade of accusations – was fined and sentenced to five months and five days in prison. Puccini settled the matter out of court with the Manfredis to avoid the shame of his wife going to prison.

Ten operas inspired by Orlando Furioso

The stories contained in Ariosto's epic sixteenth-century poem *Orlando Furioso* has inspired some 100 different operas, more than any other literary work.

1. *Angelica Delusa da Ruggero* (1725) by Albinoni
2. *Orlando Paladino* (1782) by Haydn
3. *Orlando* (1733) by Handel
4. *Ariodante* (1735) by Handel
5. *Alcina* (1735) by Handel
6. *Roland* (1685) by Lully
7. *Il Palazzo Incantato* (1642) by Rossi
8. *Orlando Finto Pazzo* (1714) by Vivaldi
9. *Orlando Furioso* (1727) by Vivaldi
10. *Ginevra* (1736) by Vivaldi

Carmen on celluloid

Since cinema began, the story of *Carmen* has fascinated film-makers, inspiring more than 70 films, including some 40 silent movie versions. Cecil B. de Mille cast Metropolitan opera star Geraldine Farrar in the 1915 version, although not a single note was heard from her. Carmen has been played by such luminaries as Theda Bara in *Carmen* (1915), Dolores Del Rio in *The Loves of Carmen* (1927), Rita Hayworth in *The Loves of Carmen* (1948), porn actress Uta Levka in *Carmen, Baby* (1967) and Beyoncé Knowles in *Carmen: A Hip Hopera* (2001). In Charlie Chaplin's *Burlesque on Carmen* (1916) Don José is reinvented as 'Darn Hosiery'. In the all-black *Carmen Jones* (1954), Dorothy Dandridge's singing part was dubbed by a 19-year-old music student called Marilyn Horne who was paid $300 for her role. A 1983 flamenco version by Carlos Saura was a big success, while *U-Carmen e-Khayelitsha* (2005) set the opera in modern-day South African township. In *Babe* (1995), the story of a pig that wants to be a sheepdog, a trio of mice sing the 'Toreador Song'.

Franz the failure

Franz Schubert (1797–1827) was probably the greatest composer never to write a good opera, despite trying his hand at 14 of them. A huge admirer of Rossini, Schubert put a lot of time and energy into writing operas but the creation of convincing musical-drama seems to have completely eluded him, except through the medium of short songs and song cycles. Of his sixteen operas, only three were staged during his lifetime. Just one of them – *Fierrabras* (1823) – has any kind of exposure today, although it only received its première 70 years after Schubert's death. Today, the beauty of much of the music in Schubert's operas is just being rediscovered.

Twenty opera singers who have appeared on the cover of Time *Magazine*

1. Nellie Melba, 18 April 1927
2. Geraldine Farrar, 5 December 1927
3. Maria Jeritza, 12 November 1928
4. Lucrezia Bori, 30 June 1930
5. Mary Garden, 15 December 1930
6. Rosa Ponselle, 9 November 1931
7. Lily Pons, 17 October 1932 and 30 December 1940
8. Lawrence M. Tibbett, 16 January 1933
9. Lotte Lehmann, 18 February 1935
10. Kirsten Flagstad, 23 December 1935
11. Lauritz Melchior, 22 January 1940
12. Helen Traubel, 11 November 1946
13. Marian Anderson, 30 December 1946
14. Mario Lanza, 6 August 1951
15. Patrice Munsel, 3 December 1951
16. Maria Callas, 29 October 1956
17. Renata Tebaldi, 3 November 1958
18. Leontyne Price, 10 March 1961
19. Beverly Sills, 22 November 1971
20. Luciano Pavarotti, 24 September 1979

Lost the Plot

The 40 most amazing opera plots

27. *Polyeucte* (1878) by Charles Gounod.
In third century Armenia, Pauline dreams that her aristocratic husband, Polyeucte, has been baptised and then struck to death by Jupiter. When he gets home, she's horrified to learn he's beginning to sympathise with the persecuted Christians. An imperial Roman general, Severe, arrives in town. He's lost touch with Pauline but still has feelings for her after a failed engagement. Polyeucte is presented to Severe and he's shocked to learn he's Pauline's husband. In a heathen temple, Severe accosts Pauline but she asks him not to see her again. Lurking in the shadows. Severe witnesses our hero converting to Christianity. At Pauline's father's home, a high priest says Jupiter will bring down his vengeance upon the Christians. Severe says that he witnessed a VIP being baptised but doesn't reveal his name. Polyeucte, who's also there, thanks Severe for his generosity but says he would be happy to die for his faith. Later as a group of Christians are being led to their execution, Polyeucte rushes in to the temple, declares he is a Christian and curses the false gods of Rome. Pauline says she is ready to die for her husband if he will renounce his Faith. Polyeucte tries to convert her so they can be united after death. Severe offers our hero the means to escape but he refuses. Our hero is taken to the arena to die. Pauline runs to join him declaring she has embraced the Christian faith. They sing the Credo together and are led to their deaths.

The Richard Wagner Fan Club – not

"Wagner is the Puccini of music."
Attributed to J.B. Morton (1893–1979)

"Of all the affected, sapless, soulless, beginningless,
endless, topless, bottomless, topsiturviest, tuneless,
scrannel-pipiest, tongs and boniest doggerel of
sounds I ever endured the deadliest of, that eternity
of nothing was the deadliest..."
John Ruskin (1819–1900) on *Die Meistersingers*

"One cannot judge *Lohengrin* from a first hearing,
and I certainly do not intend to hear it a second
time."
Gioacchino Rossini (1792–1868)

"Mr. Wagner has beautiful moments, but bad
quarter of an hours."
Attributed to Gioacchino Rossini (1792–1868)

"That old poisoner."
Claude Debussy (1862–1918)

"After the last notes of *Götterdämmerung* I felt as
though I had been let out of prison."
Píotr Ilyich Tchaikovsky (1840–1893)

"Wagner's music is better than it sounds."
Mark Twain (1835–1910)

On *Parsifal:* "The first act of the three occupied two
hours, and I enjoyed that in spite of the singing."
Mark Twain (1835–1910)

On *Parsifal:* "The kind of opera that starts at six
o'clock and after it has been going three hours you
look at your watch and it says six-twenty."
David Randolph, conductor

"I like Wagner's music better than anybody's. It is
so loud that one can talk the whole time without
other people hearing what one says."
Oscar Wilde (1854–1900) in
The Picture of Dorian Gray

"Is Wagner a human being at all? Is he not rather a
disease? He contaminates everything he touches –
he has made music sick. I postulate this viewpoint:
Wagner's art is diseased."
Friedrich Nietzche (1844–1900)

Lost the Plot

The 40 most amazing opera plots

28. *The Queen of Spades* (1890) by Pyotr Il'yich Tchaikovsky.
In a St.Petersburg park, Gherman – a soldier – notices Lisa who is unhappily engaged to Prince Yeletsky. Lisa's grandmother the Countess was famous for her card playing and trading her favours for a winning formula from an old Count. Only two men ever knew the secret because a mysterious voice warned her to beware a third who'd try to force it from her. Gherman wants to learn it. Lisa is stirred by the way Gherman looked at her in the park. He appears on her balcony, saying he's going to shoot himself because of her engagement to Yeletsky. They end up in each other's arms. Lisa slips him a key for a liaison the next day. But he goes back that night and finds the old lady asleep. She wakes up in horror. He threatens her with a pistol and she dies of fright. Lisa's distraught that her lover was more interested in the Countess's card-playing formula than her. The old woman's ghost appears to Gherman saying she must tell him the secret so he can marry and save Lisa. But when he meets Lisa, he rants so much about the formula that, spurned, she throws herself into the river. Gherman arrives at a game and starts winning, but is confronted at the end with Yeletsky playing the winning card. Granny's ghost has triumphed and Gherman loses everything – so he kills himself.

Principal conductors and music directors of La Scala, Milan

Arturo Toscanini (1898–1908)
Tullio Serafin, (1909–14)
Tullio Serafin, (1917–18)
La Scala closed from 1918 to 1920
Arturo Toscanini, (1921–29)
Victor de Sabata, (1929–53)
Carlo Maria Giulini, (1953–56)
Guido Cantelli, (1956) (Died in an airplane crash one
    week after his appointment)
No music director between 1956 and 1968
Claudio Abbado, (1968–86)
Riccardo Muti, (1986–2005)
Daniel Barenboim, (2006–) (as Principal Guest
    Conductor)

Singers on celluloid

The American soprano Grace Moore (1898–1947) became a major film star in the 1930s. *One Night of Love* (1934) was a huge success and won her an Oscar nomination. At a party hosted by Edward G. Robinson where Moore was asked to sing the title song for the guests, George Burns turned to Jack Benny and told him that it would be very rude of him to laugh when Moore started singing. Naturally as soon as she began, Benny burst out laughing. Burns announced, "See, I don't make Jack Benny laugh... Grace Moore makes Jack Benny laugh."

The film career of Mario Lanza (1921–59) began with *That Midnight Kiss* (1949) in which he played a singing truck driver. The Austrian tenor Richard Tauber (1892–1948) popped up playing Franz Schubert in *Blossom Time* (1934) in which he loses his beloved to a Count, despite his beautiful singing. In *Heart's Desire* (1935), Tauber loses his girlfriend for a second time – to a composer.

Danish-born tenor Lauritz Melchior (1890–1973), pops up in a couple of Esther Williams swimming movies, *Thrill of a Romance* (1945) and *This Time for Keeps* (1947).

American mezzo Gladys Swarthout (1904–69) appeared as a Zorro-like vigilante in *Rose of the Rancho* (1935), in which she plays a masked character who leads the ranchers in their bid to defeat the bad guys.

Luciano Pavarotti's one and only venture into film was in the box office flop *Yes, Giorgio* (1982), an ill-judged attempt to turn him into a Mario Lanza for the 1980s. Pavarotti plays tenor Giorgio Fini who loses his voice during an American tour and ends up falling in love with his throat specialist. The singing was good though.

Lost the Plot

The 40 most amazing opera plots

29. *The Rake's Progress* **(1951) by Igor Stravinsky.**
Tom, a simple fellow, has come into a huge inheritance from an unknown uncle and leaves his beloved Anne behind in the country. He heads off to the city with a mysterious stranger Nick Shadow who introduces him to a hedonistic lifestyle. Anne hears nothing from Tom and decides to go and find him. When she arrives in the city she discovers the men behaving badly. Tom has married a bearded circus performer called Baba the Turk. But Tom grows bored of his debauched lifestyle and Nick Shadow helps him launch an invention – a machine that turns stones into bread. The business ruins Tom and he has to auction everything including his wife. Baba tells Anne that she should try to save Tom, who still loves her. Shadow leads Tom to a graveyard and tells him he must end his life by midnight. But he offers a reprieve – they'll gamble for Tom's soul. Tom calls upon Anne to save him. Her voice is heard in the distance. Shadow loses the bet but condemns Tom to a life of insanity. In an asylum, Tom thinks Venus will visit him and Anne arrives to sing him to sleep before leaving him forever. All the cast gather to tell the morals drawn from the story, including that all men are mad and that the devil finds work for idle hands.

Ten operas based on works by Lord Byron

The works of Lord Byron (1788–1824) have inspired some 50 operas. The author himself makes an appearance as a character in *Mer de Glace* by Meale and *Lord Byron* by Thomson.

1. *I Due Foscari* (1844) by Verdi, inspired by *The Two Foscari*
2. *Parisina d'Este* (1833) by Donizetti, inspired by *Parisina*
3. *Marino Faliero* (1835) by Donizetti, inspired by *Marino Faliero*
4. *Torquata Tasso* (1833) by Donizetti, inspired by *The Lament of Tasso*
5. *Il Diluvio Universale* (1830) by Donizetti, inspired by *Heaven and Earth*
6. *Il Corsaro* (1848) by Verdi, inspired by *The Corsair*
7. *Manfredo* (1872) by Petrella, inspired by *Manfred*
8. *La Sposa d'Abido* (1845) by Poniatowski, inspired by *The Bride of Abydos*
9. *Caino* (1957) by Lattuada, inspired by *Cain*
10. *Hedy* (1896) by Fibich, inspired by *Don Juan*

Divine composition

"(*The Magic Flute*) is the only (opera) in
existence that might conceivably have been
composed by God."

Neville Cardus, in the
Manchester Guardian 1961

"Rossini wrote the first and last acts of *William Tell*.
God wrote the second act."

Gaetano Donizetti (1797–1848),
quoted in Osborne, *Rossini*, 1986

Lost the Plot

The 40 most amazing opera plots

30. *Rusalka* (1901) by Antonín Dvořák.
This is the story of Rusalka, a water-nymph who falls in love with a prince who often comes to the forest to swim in the lake which she is a part of. Taking the form of a wave she's embraced him, but she longs to become a human so that he might see her and give her a hug in return. Also, she's feeling grumpy about being damp all the time and wants to live in bipedal bliss in the sunshine. Her father tells her humans are full of sin but she replies, they are full of love! Rusalka sings a song to the moon, begging it to tell the Prince of her love. Not very bright this girl. A witch tells Rusalka that if she turns her into a human she will lose the power of speech and – if she is betrayed by her lover, both of them will be eternally damned. Rusalka insists and drinks the magic potion, which turns her into a beautiful, mute maiden. The prince spots her and is captivated.

By the day of the wedding, though, the Prince has already decided that a foreign princess is something of a catch and he deserts Rusalka. She throws herself back into the pond where she's told she can save herself if she spills the blood of the man who has betrayed her. The Prince comes to find her. Rusalka still loves him and gives him a smacker on the lips. He dies before she takes up her new life as a demon of death among the frog-spawn.

Renata Scotto on Maria Callas

"Listen to me, everyone speak about Callas. But I know Callas. I know Callas before she was Callas. She was fat and she had this *vociaccia* – you know what a *vociaccia* is? You go kill a cat and record its scream. She had this bad skin. And she had this rich husband. We laugh at her, you know that? And then, I sat in on a rehearsal with Maestro Serafin. You know, it was *Parsifal* and I was supposed to see if I do one of the flowers. I didn't. And she sing that music. In Italian of course. And he tell her this and he tell her that and little by little this voice had all the nature in it – the forest and the magic castle and hatred that is love. And little by little she not fat with bad skin and rich-husband-asleep-in-the-corner; she witch who burn you by standing there. Maestro Serafin he say to me afterwards, you know now something about *Parsifal*. I say, 'No, Maestro, I know much more. I know how to study. And I know that we are more than voices. We are spirit, we are God when we sing, if we mean it.' Oh yes, they will go on about Tebaldi this and Freni that. Beautiful, beautiful voices, amazing. They work hard. They sincere. They suffer. They more talented than Maria, sure. But she was the genius. Genius come from *genio* – spirit. And that make her more than all of us. So I learn from that. Don't let them take from you because you are something they don't expect. Work and fight and work and give, and maybe once in a while you are good."

Renata Scotto (1934–) in a recorded conversation with music critic Albert Innaurato.

The Classic FM Hall of Fame

Each year over Easter weekend, the UK national radio station Classic FM counts down its Hall of Fame, the Top 300 all-time favourite pieces of classical music, voted for by its audience. Votes for a particular operatic aria, overture or interlude, are amalgamated into one chart entry for the complete work from which it comes. In truth, many operas are famous for just one extract so, for example, it is the 'Pearl Fishers' Duet' that propels Bizet's opera to the top of the list. In 2007, the operas in the Hall of Fame were:

No. 33 . . . . Bizet – *The Pearl Fishers*
No. 40 . . . . Mascagni – *Cavalleria Rusticana*
No. 68 . . . . Mozart – *The Magic Flute*
No. 77 . . . . Verdi – *Nabucco*
No. 83 . . . . Mozart – *The Marriage of Figaro*
No. 89 . . . . Wagner – *Tannhäuser*
No. 92 . . . . Puccini – *Madame Butterfly*
No. 95 . . . . Puccini – *La Bohème*
No. 117 . . . . Massenet – *Thaïs*
No. 122 . . . . Wagner – *Tristan und Isolde*
No. 125 . . . . Verdi – *La Traviata*
No. 139 . . . . Dvorak – *Rusalka*
No. 140 . . . . Borodin – *Prince Igor*
No. 164 . . . . Puccini – *Gianni Schicchi*
No. 169 . . . . Verdi – *Aida*
No. 174 . . . . Wagner – *Die Walküre*
No. 180 . . . . Bizet – *Carmen*

ran Teatre del Liceu, Barcelona. Barcelona's opera
se was damaged by fire in 1861 but promptly
ilt. In November 1893, an anarchist threw two
bs into the stalls, killing some twenty members of
audience. In January 1994, it was completely
royed by fire.

ational Theatre of Prague. Opened in June 1881 to
our the visit of Crown Prince Rudolf of Austria, just
en performances followed before it closed again so
finishing touches could be made to the new
ding. During the work, a fire broke out which
royed the copper dome, auditorium and stage.

Petruzzelli, Bari. The 88-year-old opera house was
royed in October 1991.

Regio, Turin. The outstanding 1740 building was
royed by fire in 1936. It was rebuilt only in 1973.

eipzig. The theatre where Gustav Mahler conducted
destroyed along with all of Leipzig's theatres in an
aid on 3 December 1943.

Opera House. The Irish venue, built in 1855,
ived the burning of much of the city by British
es in 1920. In 1955, it succumbed after a blaze was
ed by old wiring.

est Opera. The main opera house in Romania was
aged in an earthquake in 1940 and then destroyed
ombs in 1944. The new opera house opened
53.

e Staatstheater. Built in 1851, this German opera
re was destroyed in the Second World War and
ilt in 1954.

atro Carlo Felice, Genoa. Genoa's principal opera

No. 189	Delius – *Koanga*
No. 195	Mozart – *Cosi fan Tutte*
No. 207	Rossini – *William Tell*
No. 214	Gluck – *Orpheus and Euridice*
No. 222	Britten – *Peter Grimes*
No. 225	Bellini – *Norma*
No. 228	Delibes – *Lakme*
No. 234	Handel – *Xerxes*
No. 251	Rossini – *The Thieving Magpie*
No. 258	Wagner – *Die Meistersinger*
No. 260	Puccini – *Tosca*
No. 263	Delius – *A Village Romeo and Juliet*
No. 286	Puccini – *Turandot*
No. 287	Purcell – *Dido and Aeneas*
No. 293	Mozart – *Don Giovanni*
No. 299	Offenbach – *The Tales of Hoffman*

Lost the Plot

The 40 most amazing opera plots

31. *Semele* (1744) by George Frideric Handel.
The King of Thebes's daughter, Semele is getting married to Athamas. Juno, the goddess of marriage and wife of Jupiter, gives her blessing but Semele is unhappy because she's in love with Jupiter who is a bit of a God. And what's more her sister Ino is in love with Athamas! Suddenly a roll of thunder is heard. It's the anger of Jupiter. Semele is carried off and transported to Jupiter's realm where she'll enjoy endless pleasure and endless love. His wife Juno gets cross. She vows to destroy their happiness and recruits Somnus, the god of sleep to help her. In paradise, Semele is feeling lonely and wishes she was back home. Somnus sinks Jupiter into a lustful dream of Semele and brainwashes him to grant her any wish when he wakes up. Juno disguises herself as Ino and asks Semele whether she's been granted immortality, saying that if she sees Jupiter in his true form, she will become a goddess. Jupiter returns and Semele complains he never grants any of her requests. Jupiter says he'll grant her any wish and she asks that he appear in his godlike form. But Jupiter knows that Semele won't survive such a revelation. He has to appear though in all his majesty – and Semele dies.

Burning down the house –
rise from the a

La Scala, Milan. The first theatre o
the Teatro Regio Ducale – was de
carnival gala in February 1776. I
the Second World War, its rep
damaged by bombing.

Kaiserslautern Opera. The first ope
the German city burnt down in
opening. A replacement theatre
was destroyed in the Second Wor

The Royal Opera House, Coven
House caught fire in Septembe
Handel's own organ and many
replacement was destroyed by a b
a masked ball in March 1856.

The Khedivial Opera House in Ca
world première of Verdi's *Aida* wa
in October 1971. Nothing remai

Teatro La Fenice, Venice. "The Ph
destroyed and rebuilt. Previously,
in Venice, the San Benedetto The
ground in 1774. La Fenice, built
by fire in December 1836. It was
be destroyed again in January
were found guilty of setting it
company was facing heavy fines
work.

house was hit by a shell from a British warship in February 1941 resulting in a large hole in its elaborate rococo roof. Two years later, incendiary bombs started a backstage fire that destroyed all the scenery and wooden fittings. An air raid in September 1944 destroyed the front of the theatre.

Teatro Comunale di Bologna. Much of the stage area was destroyed by fire in 1831, delaying its reopening until 1935.

Brunswick Staatstheater. The Landestheater was destroyed in World War II, replaced in 1948.

Teatro Comunale Florence. The open-air theatre was shut down after a blaze in 1864. It acquired a roof 18 years later.

Kassel Staatstheater. The 129-year-old theatre was bombed in 1943. It was replaced sixteen years later.

Teatro Donizetti, Bergamo. Built in 1791, the opera house burnt down in 1797. It reopened two years later.

The Royal Opera House, Valletta. The Maltese opera house suffered a blaze in 1873 just six years after opening. The exterior was undamaged but the interior stonework calcified. The rebuilt opera house was destroyed in 1942 by German bombs. It remains derelict.

The Bolshoi Theatre, Moscow. The current Bolshoi Theatre replaced the Petrovka Theatre that had been destroyed by fire in 1805. Extensive damage was caused in 1853. It was also hit by a bomb in World War II.

The Mariinsky Theatre, St. Petersburg. The predecessor of the Mariinsky was a wooden Equestrian circus, also used as a theatre. It burned down in 1859.

The Aktientheater, Zurich. The original 1834 Aktientheater burned down in 1890.

Teatro di San Carlo, Naples. The home of Neapolitan opera was destroyed in February 1816 but rebuilt within ten months.

Berlin State Opera. East Berlin's principal opera house was destroyed in World War II and rebuilt in 1954.

Kiev Opera. In February1896, after a performance of *Eugene Onegin*, an unextinguished candle caused a blaze which consumed the whole building in several hours. One of Europe's largest musical libraries was lost along with numerous costumes and props.

Bonn Opera House. Seventy firefighters fought the blaze at Bonn's Opera House in August 2004. Welding during roof repairs started the fire which caused around $400,000 worth of damage.

Snape Maltings Concert Hall. The original building at the heart of Benjamin Britten's Aldeburgh Festival burnt down in 1969 after the opening night of the festival. It was redesigned by Ove Arup.

Grand Théâtre, Geneva. The 71-year-old Grand Theatre burnt down in 1951, but was rebuilt the following year.

Grand Théâtre Graslin, Nantes. The Opera House opened in 1788, burnt down eight years later, and reopened after rebuilding in 1813.

Statdttheater Augsburg. The Bavarian opera house was destroyed by allied bombing in 1944, and reopened in 1956.

Bremen Opera. The original Staatstheater was destroyed in the war. Its successor opened in 1950.

Dortmund Stadttheater. Destroyed by bombs in 1943, reopened in 1966.

Kiel Stadttheater. The Schleswig-Holstein theatre was built in 1841 and destroyed by bombing in 1944. It reopened in 1953.

Lost the Plot

The 40 most amazing opera plots

32. *The Silken Ladder* **(1812) by Gioacchino Rossini.**

With the approval of an aunt, Giulia has secretly married Dorvil. But her guardian Dormont does not like Dorvil and knowing nothing of her nuptials, plans to marry her off to Dorvil's friend Blansac – who's very vain. Every night Dorvil has to climb to Giulia's balcony to see her. Giulia plots to turn Blansac's affection for her towards her cousin Lucilla. She enlists the help of her hapless servant – there's always one – without explaining what she wants. Blansac arrives, triumphant about winning Giulia's hand. The servant overhears Giulia musing about a rendezvous and thinks she is talking of meeting up with Blansac. The servant congratulates Blansac on his good fortune and Blansac is delighted. The servant also tells Lucilla all about it, and they decide to hide in Guilia's apartment to learn the ways of love. At midnight, Dorvil arrives, but then hides himself as Blansac appears at the window, who in turn conceals himself when the guardian Dormont, also pops up to find out what all the racket is. Dormont discovers all the characters lurking in their various hiding places. Giulia comes clean and tells the secret of her marriage. Dumbfounded Blansac agrees to marry Lucilla and all celebrate their good luck.

Capoul's coiffure

Joseph Victor Amadée Capoul (1839–1924) was a popular French tenor, best known for his roles as Roméo in Gounod's *Roméo et Juliette* and Auber's *Fra Diavolo*. Capoul sported a unique hairstyle, centre-parted and flattened down in curls at the front and swept up around the sides and back, resembling Wolverine in the *X-Men* movies. Such was the passion for his hairstyle that in Leo Tolstoy's short story *The death of Ivan Ilyich*, one of the characters – Fyodor Dmitryevich – has even had "his hair curled *à la Capoul*."

It's reported that the tenor himself once went to the barber and asked for his hair to be fashioned *à la Capoul*. The barber, oblivious to who was in his chair, told his customer that his head was not the right shape for that style and suggested something more like the hairstyle of Capoul's rival – the Polish tenor Jean de Reszke. To add injury to insult, Capoul had to give up the title role of Roméo to de Reszke at the Met, and played Tybalt instead.

How wrong they were . . .

"*La bohème,* even as it leaves little impression on
the minds of the audience, will leave no great trace
upon the history of our lyric theatre, and it will be
well if the composer will return to the straight road
of art, persuading himself that this has been a
brief deviation."

Carlo Bersezio, writing in *La Stampa*

"Rigoletto lacks melody. This opera has hardly any
chance of being kept in the repertoire."

Gazette musicale de Paris

Phantoms of the opera

While the world-famous Phantom who stalks the Paris Opera House is a fiction, it seems that most opera houses and theatres have an array of ghostly inhabitants.

Staff at the Cresco Opera House, Iowa report that something spooky tampers with their lighting and projection equipment. Shadowy figures have been spotted lurking around the basement and strange noises and voices have been heard.

The Opera House at Woodstock, Illinois is apparently home to a spirit named Elvira. She is believed to have been a beautiful actress who was devastated when she didn't get a part she had set her heart on, and committed suicide by, variously, jumping from the tower of the theatre, or hanging herself, or throwing herself from the fly grid. Elvira apparently favours seat DD113 in the theatre, which has been seen to lower by itself. Strange sounds have also been heard coming from the seat. Perhaps it needs oiling.

In Van Buren, Arkansas, it is said that a young actor was whipped to death after he tried to elope with the daughter of a local doctor who caught up with him. The actor's ghost has been sighted at Van Buren's King Opera House, dressed in a top-hat and a long cape.

The Grand Opera House in Oshkosh, Wisconsin is full of ghosts. The spirit of Percy Keene, a former stage manager, has been sighted watching over the theatre. An apparition has been spotted in an underground passage and an unseen hand once grabbed the ankle of a production assistant. Staff talk of lights turning on and off, sudden temperature drops and sounds that cannot be explained.

The Springer Opera House in Columbus, Georgia has been named one of the "Ten Most Haunted Places in America". The laughter of children can often be heard upstairs in the dressing room. The most famous and frequent visitor is the spirit of Edwin Booth, the renowned Shakespearean actor, which has appeared onstage, in box seats and in the lobby where his portrait hangs.

Lost the Plot

The 40 most amazing opera plots

33. *La Sonnambula* (1831) by Vincenzo Bellini.
Lisa – a village landlady has been engaged to Elvino. But he's dumped her for Amina. At their engagement party, a stranger called Rodolfo arrives. Lisa invites him to stay the night at her inn. The locals say there's a mysterious woman who haunts the village every night. Late at the inn, Rodolfo starts to flirt with Lisa but their fun and games are curtailed! The phantom arrives. It's actually Amina, sleepwalking. Lisa runs off to tell Elvino that his betrothed is being unfaithful. They return to the Inn to find Amina sleeping in Rodolfo's room. Elvino calls off their engagement. Amina pleads her innocence but he wants his ring back. Rodolfo assures the villagers that Amina was faithful to Elvino but he decides to marry Lisa right away. Rodolfo gives a lecture on sleepwalking, but no one believes him. Lisa announces she's never set foot in a man's bedroom but one of the villagers produces a scarf that she'd left in Rodolfo's room! Elvino despairs of ever finding a wife when Amina appears again sleepwalking. In her sleep, she speaks with such conviction of her sorrow at losing Elvino that he is finally convinced of her innocence. Elvino returns the ring to her finger and she wakes up. She sings joyously of their reunion and, accompanied by Elvino and the celebrating villagers, heads to the church to be married.

Ten operas based on works by Sir Walter Scott

The novels and poems of Sir Walter Scott (1771–1832) have been the inspiration for some 60 operas, particularly from Italian composers of the early nineteenth century.

1. *Lucia di Lammermoor* (1835) by Donizetti, inspired by *The Bride of Lammermoor*
2. *La Jolie Dille de Perth* (1867) by Bizet, inspired by *The Fair Maid of Perth*
3. *Ivanhoe* (1891) by Sullivan, inspired by *Ivanhoe*
4. *La Donna del Lago* (1819) by Rossini, inspired by *The Lady of the Lake*
5. *I Puritani* (1835) by Bellini, inspired by *Old Morality*
6. *Rob Roy* (1836) by Flotow, inspired by *Rob Roy*
7. *La Dame Blanche* (1825) by Boïeldieu, inspired by *Guy Mannering*
8. *La Prigione d'Edimburgo* (1838) by Ricci, inspired by *The Heart of Midlothian*
9. *Il Castello di Kenilworth* (1829) by Donizetti, inspired by *Kenilworth*
10. *König Richard in Palästina* (1827) by Riotte, inspired by *The Talisman*

The final frontier – operas in outer space

Il Mondo della luna (1750) by Baldassare Galuppi (1706–85). A fake astronomer claims he has a powerful telescope which can see not only a world on the moon but can also detect its inhabitants, their homes, and women undressing as they go to bed.

The Excursions of Mr Broucek (1920) by Leos Janacek (1854–1928). Mr Broucek is whisked off to the moon where women need to be worshipped from a kneeling position, flower smells are the highest form of art and vegetarians despise his love of sausages.

Der Mond (1939) by Carl Orff (1895–1982). The moon has been commandeered by a country that is in complete darkness. Rascals decide to steal the moon and cut it into four. The parts of the moon are glued back together. It is so bright it wakes the dead. The moon is taken back into space to restore peace.

Aniara (1959) by Karl-Birger Blomdahl (1916–68). Drama set on a spaceship on its way to Mars after a nuclear explosion atomises the planet Doris. The passengers distract themselves, by dancing and practicing a sex cult called Yurg.

Help, Help, the Globolinks! (1969) by Gian-Carlo Menotti (1911–2007). The Globolinks, sinister but funny creatures from outer space, invade earth but are allergic to music.

Donnerstag aus licht (1978–1980) by Karlheinz Stoclkhausen (1928–). Michael falls in love with an extra-terrestrial bird-woman called Moon-Eve. He flies around the world as a trumpeter. He goes to heaven too.

The Making of the Representative for Planet 8 (1988) by Philip Glass (1937–). Based on a Doris Lessing novel, this opera tells the story of a planet entering an ice age. The people are guided by extra-terrestrial overlords to evolve into a one collective soul that transcends the deaths of individuals.

Lost the Plot

The 40 most amazing opera plots

34. *The Tale of Tsar Sultan* (1900) by Nikolay Rimsky-Korsakov. The Tsar of Russia overhears three sisters who confide with each other their views on the subject of happiness. One loves to cook, the other to weave and the youngest says she would like nothing better than to marry the Tsar and become the mother of a hero. She, not surprisingly, is chosen by the Tsar to be his bride while her sisters are appointed royal cook and royal weaver. Later, while the Tsar is away at war, the two jealous sisters plot against the young Queen who's sent a message to the Tsar announcing their son's birth. But the sisters intercept the message and tell the Tsar that the Queen's given birth to a monster. The Tsar is not best pleased, and orders that mother and baby be cast into the sea. They spend years drifting around in a barrel. All washed up, they arrive on an island where the Prince – Guidon – saves a Swan Princess from an attacking pike and is rewarded with a magic city, of which he becomes king. On the advice of the Princess, Guidon transforms himself into a bee, and reaches his father's court with three sailors, who tell of the marvels of Guidon's island. The Tsar wants to visit the island. Guidon ends up marrying the Swan Princess and the Tsar comes to the island where he is re-united with his wife and son, while the two horrid sisters get their just desserts.

Following the leader

Real-life political figures have popped up in operas throughout the centuries. They include:

Emperor Nero – *L'Incoronazione di Poppea* (1643) by Claudio Monteverdi

Edward III – *L'Assedio di Calais* (1836) by Gaetano Donizetti

William Wallace, Scottish nationalist in *Vallace, o L'eroe scozzee* (1820) by Giovanni Pacini, and in *Vallace* (1830) by Gioacchino Rossini

William Tell, Swiss nationalist – *Guillaume Tell* (1829) by Gioacchino Rossini

Anne Boleyn, English Queen – *Anna Bolena* (1830) by Gaetano Donizetti

Mary, Queen of Scots – *Maria Stuarda* (1835) by Gaetano Donizetti

Marguerite de Valois – *Les Huguenots* (1836) by Giacomo Meyerbeer

Attila the Hun – *Attila* (1846) by Giuseppe Verdi

King Heinrich I of Saxony – *Lohengrin* (1850) by Richard Wagner

Philip II of Spain – *Don Carlos* (1866–67) by Giuseppe Verdi

Tsar Boris Godunov – *Boris Godunov* (1868–69) by Modest Mussorgsky

Herod, King of Judea – *Salome* (1905) by Richard Strauss

Henry V – *At the Boar's Head* (1925) by Gustav Holst

Napoleon Bonaparte – *Madame Sans-Gêne* (1915) by
Umberto Giordano, *Háry János* (1926) by Zoltán
Kodály, *War and Peace* (1945) by Sergey Prokofiev,
Toussaint (1977) by David Blake

Mahatma Gandhi, Martin Luther King – *Satyagraha*
(1980) by Philip Glass

**Richard Nixon, Chairman Mao Tse-Tung, Henry
Kissinger** – *Nixon in China* (1987) by John Adams

Malcolm X – *X: The Life and Times of Malcolm X* (1989)
by Anthony Davis

Nelson Mandela – *No Easy Walk to Freedom* (1992–95)
by Chandler Carter

Colonel Muammar Gadaffi – *Gadaffi – A Living Myth*
(2006) by Asian Dub Foundation and Diaspora with
English National Opera

Henry II – *Rosmonda d'Inghilterra* by Donizetti

Edward III – *L'Assedio di Calais* by Donizetti

Five pieces of Pavarotti trivia

1. Pavarotti was a fan of Turin-based football club Juventus.
2. Pavarotti was the only classical artist to have had a
   number one hit in the UK singles charts with *Nessun
   Dorma,* used as the World Cup theme song in 1990.
3. Pavarotti fought on *Celebrity Deathmatch* with the
   other two tenors against the Three Stooges.
4. In the cartoon series, *Futurama,* Pavarotti's head was
   sacrificed in favour of protecting the head of Lucy Liu.

5. In 2004, it was reported that Pavarotti rented 15 suites at Le Royal Meridien hotel in Hamburg for his entourage. He also had a custom-built kitchen installed in his suite.

Wearing the trousers

Many leading roles in early Italian opera were assigned to be sung by castrati, men with very high, surgically enhanced, pure voices. With the decline of castrati, women were cast in their place, but were required to play men. Here are 20 famous "breeches" roles:

1. Ariodante and Lurcanio in Handel's *Ariodante*
2. Ascanio in Berlioz's *Benvenuto Cellini*
3. Cherubino in Mozart's *The Marriage of Figaro*
4. The Composer in Richard Strauss's *Ariadne auf Naxos*
5. Hansel in Humperdinck's *Hansel und Gretel*
6. Idamante in Mozart's *Idomeneo*
7. Kitchen Boy in Dvořák's *Rusalka*
8. Nicklausse in Offenbach's *The Tales of Hoffmann*
9. Oktavian in Richard Strauss's *Der Rosenkavalier*
10. Oscar in Verdi's *Un ballo in Maschera*
11. Prince Orlofsky in Johann Strauss II's *Die Fledermaus*
12. Romeo in Bellini's *I Capuleti e i Montecchi*
13. Ruggiero in Handel's *Alcina*
14. Sesto and Annio in Mozart's *La clemenza di Tito*
15. Siebel in Gounod's *Faust*

16. Stefano in Gounod's *Romeo and Juliet*
17. Tancredi and Ruggiero in Rossini's *Tancredi*
18. Urbain in Meyerbeer's *Les Huguenots*
19. Xerxes in Handel's *Xerxes*
20. Zdenka in Richard Strauss's *Arabella*

Lost the Plot

The 40 most amazing opera plots

35. *Die Tote Stadt* (1920) by Erich Wolfgang Korngold.
Paul – a widower – has never stopped mourning his wife Marie. So when he meets a dancer Marietta, who uncannily resembles Marie, he invites her to visit. When she arrives she performs a seductive dance, dislodging a curtain and revealing Marie's portrait. Paul is torn between his loyalty to Marie's memory and his desire for Marietta. Marie appears in a vision and Paul vows his fidelity. Outside Marietta's house, he encounters his friend Frank who has arrived for a tryst with Marietta. They fight and Paul grabs Marietta's door key from Frank. When Marietta returns with her troupe, she dances flirtatiously with a colleague. Paul is outraged and bursts in. He tells her he is obsessed with her. Marietta seduces him saying its time to banish the phantom of Marie. The next day, Paul tells her of his guilt. Marietta ridicules him and he strangles her. Then as it gets light, Paul is back in his room and his housekeeper announces the arrival of Marietta. The whole story has been Paul's fantasy and that he has decided not to be seduced by Marietta but to leave the dead city.

One good turn defends another

After World War II broke out, Michael Tippett (1905–1998), composer of *The Midsummer Marriage* and *King Priam*, applied to be conditionally registered as a conscientious objector. The case did not go to tribunal until 1942 when he was directed to carry out non-combatant duties. On appeal, Tippett was given conditional registration but was instructed to do some kind of approved labour, such as farm work. He refused a number of jobs, saying that the field in which he could best serve was music. He was brought to trial at Oxted Police Court on the charge of failing to comply with the conditions of his exemption. Ralph Vaughan Williams (1872–1958), composer of *Hugh the Drover* and *Sir John in Love* was called to defend Tippett and told the court, "I think Tippett's pacifist views entirely wrong, but I respect him very much for holding them so firmly. I think his compositions are very remarkable and form a distinct national asset, and will increase the prestige of this country in the world … We know music is forming a great part in national life now; more since the war than ever before, and everyone able to help with that work is doing work of national importance."

Despite Vaughan Williams's interventions, Tippet was imprisoned for three months in Wormwood Scrubs.

Lost the Plot

The 40 most amazing opera plots

36. *Il trovatore* (1857) by Giuseppe Verdi.

A long time ago in far off Aragon, a gypsy woman was burned at the stake for bewitching the baby brother of the Count DiLuna. The Gypsy's daughter kidnapped the child. Years later, the Count still hopes his brother is alive. Now the Count has the hots for Lady Leonora. So does Manrico, the troubadour. Leonora loves Manrico and the jealous Count challenges him to a duel. Meanwhile the Gypsy's daughter tells Manrico that she did not kill the Duke's brother and that it is he. She asks Manrico to avenge the death of the witch – his adoptive granny, so to speak – in the duel with the Count. Leonora decides to join a nunnery – they always do. The Count waits by the cloister to kidnap her. But Manrico rushes in and escapes with her. The Count meanwhile decides to flambé the gypsy's daughter as well. Manrico sings farewell while Leonora resolves to save him. When the Count turns up, Leonora agrees to yield to him but secretly swallows poison. Manrico comforts his mum, the witch in her cell before she's roasted alive. Leonora rushes in urging her lover to flee. Manrico takes Leonora in his arms as she dies. Furious at losing Leonora, the Count has Manrico's head chopped off. The witch staggers to her feet to see the axe fall and tell the Count that he has actually killed his own brother, thus avenging the death of her mother.

Ten operatic ways to die

1. Get pecked to death by a cockerel. King Dodon in *The Golden Cockerel* by Rimsky-Korsakov.
2. Get thrown into boiling oil by your father. Rachel in *La Juive* (1835) by Halévy.
3. Get strangled by your own hair. Chim-Fen in *L'Oracolo* by Leoni, Marietta in *Die Tote Stadt* by Korngold, and Guenièvre in *Le Roi Arthus* by Chausson.
4. Fling yourself into an erupting volcano. Fenella in *La Muette de Portici* (1828) by Auber, and Huascar in Rameau's *Les Indes Galantes*.
5. Get locked in a cupboard by your wife. Giovanni in *Mona Lisa* by Schilling.
6. Get bricked into a vault. Radamès and Aida in *Aida* by Verdi.
7. Get sown into a coffee sack and burnt alive. The forty thieves in *Ali Baba* (1833) by Cherubini.
8. Get mistaken for an otter and shot. Danny in *The Lily of Killarney* by Benedict.
9. Get in the way of an avalanche. Wally and Hagenbach in *La Wally*.
10. Get guillotined. All the nuns in *Dialogues des Carmélites* (1957) by Poulenc.

Lost the Plot

The 40 most amazing opera plots

37. *A Village Romeo and Juliet* (1910) by Frederick Delius.

Sali is the son of a farmer called Manz. Vrenchen is the daughter of another farmer called Marti. One day Sali and Vrenchen are playing on a wild plot of land. The land is rightfully owned by the mysterious Dark Fiddler but because he's illegitimate he has no legal rights over it. But he warns the children that the land must never be tilled. The two farmers argue over the land and stop their children from playing together. Six years later, a lawsuit has ruined both families. Sali and Vrenchen meet on the wild land where the Dark Fiddler appears and invites them to join him. Marti spots them and drags Vrenchen away. Sali tries to stop him and knocks him down. Marti goes mad and is taken off by the men in white coats. Sali goes to see Vrenchen at her house which is on the market at a very reasonable price. They declare their love for each other and decide to run away. At a local fair, they buy rings. Sali mentions a rundown inn called the Paradise Garden where they can dance all night. At the inn they see the Dark Fiddler who suggests they follow him into the mountains. Instead they decide their love is so great they want to die together. They climb into a hay barge and Sali removes the plug from the bottom as it moves off. Nothing like making hay while the boat sinks.

The final curtain

In 1960, the American baritone Leonard Warren was appearing on stage with the New York Metropolitan Opera in Verdi's *La Forza del Destino*. In Act III, he was about to begin the aria, 'Morir, tremenda cosa' ('To die, a momentous thing'), when he started gasping and fell to the floor. A few minutes later he was pronounced dead from a heart attack, at the age of 48. The rest of the performance was cancelled.

Raoul Laparra, French composer of the opera *La Habañera* (1908), was killed in the bombing of Boulogne-sur-Seine in 1943. Jean-Baptiste Lully, the court composer to Louis XIV, hit his foot while beating time with a stick and died later of gangrene.

The French soprano Amelia Talexis was such a hefty woman that the porcelain toilet she was sitting on in a hotel in Calais in 1911 broke under her weight, inflicting severe cuts. By the time rescuers had managed to break into the locked bathroom, the singer had died.

Fritz Wunderlich, the German tenor, broke his skull falling down the stairs at a friend's hunting lodge near Maulbronn in 1966. It's believed he tripped on the open shoestrings of his hunting boots and grabbed at the rope banister, ripping it off the wall, sending him tumbling down the stairs. He died in hospital nine days before his 36th birthday.

The American soprano Lillian Nordica was touring Australia in 1914. She almost missed a ship leaving Sydney but wired the captain asking him to wait for her. The ship waited but shortly into the voyage was wrecked on a coral reef, leaving the passengers stranded for three days. Nordica never recovered from the exposure she suffered and died in Java from 'nervous prostration' and pneumonia.

The tenor Felix Senius succumbed to food poisoning after eating oysters at a dinner being given in his honour.

Tenor Brian Sullivan drowned in Lake Geneva in 1969. He had arrived in Geneva to sing a role but discovered, on arrival, that another singer had been given his role. Italian soprano Lina Cavalieri died during the allied bombardment of her home on the outskirts of Florence, Italy.

French tenor Adolphe Nourrit, for whom Rossini wrote the role of *Le comte Ory*, committed suicide in 1839 by jumping out of a window. His fame was fading in the late 1830s as other singers became more fashionable.

The British tenor Gervase Elwes died at the age of 55 after falling under a train at the railway station in Boston, Massachusetts. The singer had been rushing back to the moving train to get the coat he had left in a carriage.

Maria Malibran, one of the greatest of all sopranos, tumbled from her horse while taking part in a hunt and suffered injuries from which she never recovered. She continued to perform using crutches, but died in 1936 five months after the fall.

Mystery surrounded the death of Nellie Melba who was an apparently healthy 70-year-old when she died in 1931. Her death certificate records that she died from septicaemia. Seven decades after her passing, it was revealed that the superstar soprano had contracted erysipelas – an acute bacterial skin infection – after an unsuccessful facelift operation.

The successful Spanish mezzo Conchita Supervia died after giving birth to a stillborn baby in 1936. In 1947, Grace Moore had just sung to an audience of 4000 in Copenhagen before the KLM DC3 plane she boarded to fly to her next concert in Stockholm crashed and exploded upon take-off.

Baritone Robert Merrill, who became known to Major League Baseball fans for his rendition of 'The Star-Spangled Banner' at the opening of every New York Yankees season for three decades, died at the age of 85 while watching the televised first game of the 2004 World Series between the Boston Red Sox and the St. Louis Cardinals. His epitaph states: "Like a bursting celestial star, he showered his family and the world with love, joy, and beauty. Encore please."

Rest in Peace

Twenty great opera singers and where they are buried.

1. Marian Anderson (1897–1993) – Eden Memorial Cemetery, Collingdale, PA, USA
2. Ettore Bastianini (1922–67) – Church of San Domenico, Siena, Italy
3. Jussi Björling (1911–60) – Stora Tuna Kyrkogård, Borlange, Sweden
4. Clara Butt (1872–1936) – St. Mary the Virgin Churchyard, North Stoke, UK
5. Franco Corelli (1921–2003) – Cimitero Monumentale, Milan, Italy

6. Nicholai Ghiaurov (1929–2004) – San Cataldo Cemetery, Modena, Italy
7. Beniamino Gigli (1890–1957) – Recanati Cemetery, Lazio, Italy
8. Jenny Lind (1820–87) – The Cemetery, Great Malvern, Worcestershire, UK
9. Lauritz Melchior (1890–1973) – Assistens Cemetery, Copenhagen, Denmark
10. Robert Merrill (1917–2004) – Sharon Gardens Cemetery, Valhalla, NY, USA
11. Zinka Milanov (1906–89) – Mirogoj Cemetery, Zagreb, Croatia
12. Birgit Nilsson (1918–2005) – Västra Karups kyrkogård, Bastad, Sweden
13. Adelina Patti (1843–1919) – Cimitière du Pére Lachaise, Paris, France
14. Luciano Pavarotti (1935–2007) – Montale Rangone Cemetery, Modena, Italy
15. Lily Pons (1904–76) – Cimitière du Grand Jas de Cannes, Cannes, France
16. Rosa Ponselle (1897–1981) – Druid Ridge Cemetery, Pikesville, MD, USA
17. Leonie Rysanek (1926–98) – Zentralfriedhof Wien, Vienna, Austria
18. Elisabeth Schwarzkopf (1915–2006) – Zumikon Friedhof, Zurich, Switzerland
19. Fiodor Shaliapin (1873–1938) – Novo-Devichy Cemetery, Moscow, Russia
20. Giuseppina Strepponi (1815–97) – Casa di Reposo per Musicisti, Milan, Italy

Lost the Plot

The 40 most amazing opera plots

38. *Le Villi* (1884) by Giacomo Puccini.
In the house of a forest guard, a lovely young couple called Roberto and Anna are celebrating their engagement. Roberto has been left a fortune and he has to travel to the big city to sort out his legal matters. Anna sees this as a bad omen, and she's right to. Everyone wishes Roberto a successful journey. Anna puts her engagement bouquet into his luggage. She's hopeful that when he looks at the flowers, he will think of her. It'll make his underwear smell nice too. In the city, it doesn't take long before Roberto is seduced by a witch, disguised as a courtesan, and sure enough, he forgets Anna. When Anna finds out, the same witch makes sure she dies of a broken heart and her soul joins a company of abandoned girls, waiting for their unfaithful lovers, who they'll dance with until they die. Anna's father, Guglielmo, mourns for his daughter. He prays that the same spirits will wreak their vengeance upon Roberto when he returns. Roberto comes back remorseful for letting himself be seduced by another woman. He is shocked to find out that his true love is now dead at the hand of the same witch. Anna's ghost appears to him, and both are surrounded by the other spirits. They oblige Roberto to dance with Anna until he dies.

Lost the Plot

The 40 most amazing opera plots

39. *La Wally* (1892) by Alfredo Catalani.
This opera is set in the mountains of the Tyrol in the early nineteenth century. La Wally is in love with a hunter called Hagenbach. However, her old man doesn't think much of Hagenbach and would rather have her marry his old chum, called Gellner. Daddy gives daughter an ultimatum: marry Gellner or get on your bike. Faced with the decision, La Wally decides she must leave. She despairs that she will never see her house again but she knows that she must be firm – or at least well supported. Hagenbach arrives with a group of friends, and boasts about killing a bear with one single shot to the poor creature's heart. La Wally is angry with Hagenbach because he doesn't return her affections. He has kissed her once, but she believes that he only kissed her to see if he could conquer her. Humiliated she swears to get revenge on him, regretting that her youthful innocence was taken by this brute of a man. Gellner's anxious to win her affections and with our heroine's encouragement, pushes Hagenbach down a ravine. However she feels a bit bad about that and she repents and jumps in to rescue him. At the bottom of the ravine, he tells her that he does love her after all … but just as it looks like they'll live happily ever after, an avalanche falls on top of them. The End.

The death of Verdi

"Verdi is dead. He has taken away with him an enormous amount of light and of vital warmth; we were all brightened by the sunshine of that Olympian old age... He died magnificently, like a formidable silenced fighter... His head bowed on his chest, his eyebrows stern, he looked down and seemed to measure with his gaze an unknown and formidable adversary, and to calculate mentally the strength required to oppose him. He also put up a heroic resistance ... poor Maestro! How good and beautiful he was to the very end ... but never before have I experienced such a feeling of hatred against death, of contempt for that mysterious, blind, stupid, triumphant and craven power. It needed the death of this octegenarian to arouse these feelings in me."

Arrigo Boito, in a letter to Camille Bellaigue.

Purcell's epitaph

Purcell's grave in London's Westminster Abbey is inscribed with the following epitaph thought to be written by Dryden, or his wife, or her sister-in-law Dame Annabella Howard who put up the monument:

Here Lyes
HENRY PVRCELL. Esq[r].
Who left his life
And is gone to that Blessed Place
Where only his Harmony
can be exceeded.

Lost the Plot

The 40 most amazing opera plots

40. *Xerxes* **(1738) by George Frideric Handel.**
A young King, who's already engaged, is pursuing another –
Romilda, determined to make her love him. But Romilda's in love
with his brother, Arsamene – sounds like a suppository. The King
banishes Arsamene. Romilda's sister, Atalanta, also has her eye on
Arsamene and makes overtures to him. Arsamene sends a letter to
Romilda but Atalanta intercepts it. She tells the King that
Arsamene loves *her* and wrote *her* the note – thus freeing the King
to pursue Romilda. The King is relentless and cruel in his pursuit
of Romilda. He tells her father, cryptically, that someone of his
family and equal to him will come to claim Romilda. The father
thinks the King means his brother Arsamene and arranges a
wedding. The lovers are reunited though this is not what the King
intended. The King's fiancée comes to town disguised as a man to
find and observe her betrothed from whom she has heard nothing.
She watches his scheming and writes him a warning. In a sudden
flash of conscience, he feels terribly ashamed and asks her to stay.
He has learned a lot from his impassioned pursuit of Romilda and
all his longing for love is now transferred to someone who'll
actually love him back. As for Atalanta, she's left alone to stew.
And they all live happily ever after – except Atalanta.

CURTAIN CALL

The author would like to call to the front of the stage and offer bouquets to a number of individuals without whose encouragement and assistance, this book would not have been possible, namely:

Lesley Garrett CBE
Darren Henley and Giles Pearman at Classic FM
Martin Liu and Pom Somkabcharti of Cyan Books
Michael Norrish
Oliver Condy at *BBC Music* magazine
Richard Leigh
Nancy Lee Harper
Sarah Abel
Ryan Jenkyns for his illustrations

BIBLIOGRAPHY

The following books have made for interesting and entertaining reading in the preparation of this book. If your appetite has been whetted, then many of the following will be of further interest to you:

Adami, Giuseppe, ed. *Letters of Giacomo Puccini*.
    Philadelphia: J.B. Lippincott, 1931.
Anderson, James. *Dictionary of Opera*. London:
    Bloomsbury, 1989.
Barber, David W. *When the Fat Lady Sings*. Toronto:
    Sound and Vision, 1990.
Boyden, Matthew. *Opera – The Rough Guide*. London:
    Rough Guides, 1997.
Forman, Denis. *The Good Opera Guide*. London: Phoenix
    Press, 2001.
Gallo, Denise. *Opera – The Basics*. Abingdon: Routledge,
    2006.
Hardcastle, Robert. *Verdi*. Staplehurst: Spellmount, 1996.
Henley, Darren and Lihoreau, Tim. *Classic Ephemera*.
    London: Boosey and Hawkes, 2005.

Mordden, Ethan. *Opera Anecdotes.* Oxford: Oxford University Press, 1985.

Norwich, John Julius. *Christmas Crackers.* London: Penguin Books, 1982.

Ramsden, Timothy. *Puccini.* Staplehurst: Spellmount, 1996.

Riding, Alan and Dunton-Downer, Leslie, eds. *Eyewitness Companion Opera.* London: Dorling Kindersley, 2006.

Rosenthal, Harold. *Covent Garden Memories and Traditions.* London: Michael Joseph, 1976.

Tanner, Stephen B. *Opera Antics and Anecdotes.* Toronto: Sound and Vision, 2005.

Tanner, Stephen and Tanner, Nancy. *Opera – Aria ready for a laugh.* Toronto: Sound and Vision, 2003.

Watson, Derek, ed. *The Wordsworth Dictionary of Musical Quotations.* Edinburgh: Wordsworth Editions, 1994.

Wlaschin, Ken. *Encyclopedia of Opera on Screen.* New Haven: Yale University Press, 2004.